Gender
Euphoria

Gender Euphoria

Stories of joy from trans, non-binary and intersex writers

edited by Laura Kate Dale

unbound

First published in 2021

Unbound
Level 1, Devonshire House, One Mayfair Place, London W1J 8AJ
www.unbound.com
All rights reserved

This book is a work of non-fiction based on the lives, experiences
and recollections of the contributors. In some cases names of
people, places, dates, sequences or the detail of events have been
changed to protect the privacy of others. Except in such minor
respects not affecting the substantial accuracy of the work, the
contents of this book are true.

Text design by PDQ Digital Media Solutions Ltd

A CIP record for this book is available from the British Library

ISBN 978-1-80018-056-7 (paperback)
ISBN 978-1-80018-057-4 (ebook)

Printed and bound in Great Britain by Clays Ltd, Elcograf S.p.A.

5   7   9   8   6

Contents

Introduction

So often, when we see pop-culture portrayals of trans and non-cisgender people's lives, hear stories shared by trans people about their transitions, or accounts by the media about trans people and their transitions, those stories focus on misery and discomfort.

It makes sense why this happens. For many transgender people, a big part of what initially pushes us to realise we need to come out is experiencing gender dysphoria, an unpleasant feeling of disconnect between our gender assigned at birth, and our own knowledge of our lived experience. Maybe you hit puberty and start growing facial hair, or your voice drops, or you start growing breasts, and suddenly you feel uncomfortable, like the changes happening to your body are alien, are transforming you into someone you don't want to be. All those quietly held thoughts about not being your birth-assigned gender you might have grown up with suddenly have a focal point: your body is changing and you don't like what it's becoming.

Not every trans person experiences dysphoria, and it's certainly not required to be valid as a trans person, but there's a reason it gets talked about so often, and it is used as part of diagnostic criteria. It's quite often what kicks a person from spending years thinking, *It sure would be nice to be a different gender from the one I was assigned at birth*, into actually deciding to make a change in who they want to live as. Gender dysphoria is a catalyst: it lights a fire under many and underscores the aspects of themselves they're unhappy living with.

Trans people all around the world today, to greater or lesser degrees, are still fighting for legal recognition of their gender status, legal protections, rights and safety. When it comes to explaining why you need the right to live the way you do, that you feel uncomfortable with yourself, that you need to alleviate a pain deeply lodged in you, that's easy to explain quickly and simply. Everyone has been hurt emotionally in their lives, and it's easy to understand why you would want to take steps to avoid that discomfort.

Beyond that, even, the media plays a part in that framing of the trans narrative. If you want people to feel sympathy for the trans community, explain we're escaping dysphoria. If you want to demonise the community, tell people our dysphoria is a delusion and shouldn't be indulged. It can be spun differently depending on who's trying to spin it, which makes it a powerful aspect of the way trans stories are so often portrayed.

I know I, as a trans person, fall into this trap sometimes when discussing my own transition. When I wrote my memoir a few years ago, sure, it touched on some positives and joyful moments, but that certainly wasn't the focus. I wrote a lot about not fitting in growing up, about struggling to be accepted when I came out, and I wrote about the challenges I am facing in the world today. It made sense to share those parts of my story with the world, but it also got me thinking about how prevalent that narrative can be when discussing trans stories.

Over the couple of years since then, I have thought a lot about the importance of celebrating the fact that stories of transition are not all just about doom and gloom, as much as it may sometimes feel that way. I've experienced countless moments of elation, pride, confidence, freedom and ecstasy as a direct result of my coming out as a trans woman the better part of a decade ago, and I know I am not alone. When I talk to my trans, non-binary, agender, gender-fluid and intersex friends, I have heard countless wonderful stories about the ways that coming to terms with gender brought unimaginable happiness and love into their lives.

When I said earlier that gender dysphoria isn't a required part of being trans, I meant it. When I say that, sometimes people ask me how someone would know they were trans, if not for feeling uncomfortable with their body and the way they were born. And to that, I say the answer is simple. If you try presenting yourself as something other than your birth-assigned gender, and it makes you feel euphoric, that's just as valid a reason to claim your identity as escaping dysphoria. Gender euphoria is an equally valid reason to decide who you are.

I'm not going to pretend that the world isn't sometimes a bit miserable for non-cisgender people. I'm not going to pretend a lot of us didn't have a rough road to get where we are now. But, this book isn't about that. This book is about gender euphoria. This book is about people doing small actions and grand gestures that made them feel radiantly themselves and wonderfully at peace. This book is about stories of transition as euphoria.

So, before we go any further, who am I? Well, my name is Laura Kate Dale. I am a twenty-nine-year-old pansexual trans woman author of three books, full-time video-game critic and podcaster. Of the essays contained in this anthology, I wrote around one third of them, with the rest being written by a wonderful list of contributing authors.

Over the next 70,000 words or so, you'll read several essays about my own experiences with gender euphoria throughout the past decade, but you'll also read essays from a vast array of non-cisgender writers of different orientations and backgrounds, and with a varied selection of experiences to share. Every author hand-picked to contribute an essay to this anthology was selected above hundreds of other writers because I felt they had a uniquely joyful story to tell and was excited to help them tell that story to the world. From an agender dominatrix getting called Daddy, to an Arab trans man getting his first tattoos in spite of cultural taboo, a non-binary intersex writer not having to choose between puberties and a trans woman embracing her inner fighter, this book will take you on a journey through how coming to terms with who you are can be about more than avoiding someone you don't want to be.

4

So, thank you for picking up this book. I hope you feel as overjoyed reading it as I felt having the privilege to put it together.

Laura Kate Dale, 2020

Becoming Prom King: How My Classmates Showed Their Support for My Transition

Oliver Jones

Eighteen, a transgender man from England

Trans people can often get swept up into the mindset that until you have completed your transition (socially, medically, legally), your life is on hold. You are forever waiting for things to fall into place.

I came out as a trans boy to my family and peers at school when I was thirteen years old.

A few months before, my teachers were so concerned about my behaviour at school that they recommended I see the on-site counsellor. I was refusing to take part in class, getting into fights with other kids, having screaming matches with my teachers. I hated everything and I didn't care if my grades dropped or I got kicked out. Something was wrong, but I couldn't pinpoint what it was. I just felt angry with the world.

I explained this to the school therapist. I did not expect her to tell me she suspected I might have gender dysphoria. I had no idea what being that meant. But when it was explained to me, I knew I fit the description.

I was the textbook trans guy. I refused to wear dresses. I begged my mum to let me have short hair and buy clothes from the boys' section. I only played with the boys at school, and I wanted nothing to do with the girls. I spent my free time playing video games, football, skateboarding and running around outside. When my poor behaviour at school was called out by teachers and counsellors, I told them I wished I was a boy. That was the only explanation I could give. In hindsight, that was a pretty big clue as to what was going on.

Suddenly the strange childhood that I'd spent resenting my biology made total sense. The counsellor told me she'd seen other trans students whose experiences were similar to mine. She said she could see I presented myself in a very masculine way, even if I wasn't aware of it, and she asked me if I thought I might be transgender.

For me there was no confusion, no internal struggle or conflict. I didn't stop to think about how hard the journey would be, or how I'd probably become a laughing stock, the butt of every joke, turning heads as the other kids at school sniggered at me when I walked past.

All I knew was that, for the first time in my life, there was the chance for me to be happy and confident in who I was. I do think it's important to highlight that it wasn't so much my fear of being a woman that drove me to transition. It was my desperate yearning to be a man.

As early as I can remember, I lay awake at night wondering why I hated being female so much. I'd look at every boy I saw in public, at the park, at school, and

8

wish I could be him. I told anyone who'd listen that I didn't want to be a girl, but I didn't know transition was an option, so I accepted that my destiny was to be sad, insecure and unhappy forever.

At the time, finding out that I didn't have to live as a girl didn't feel like a life-changing, enlightening moment. I know some trans folks describe it as something they'll never forget, something that instantly clicked with them and brought them joy as they finally found the right description for what they'd been feeling. Well, I've never been very emotional or expressive, and it was just a fact that I accepted. 'Transgender people exist.' It wasn't exactly world-shattering. But the real truth that I'd discovered was 'transgender people exist, and I am one of them'.

From the moment I knew I was trans, I had to come out. I spent a long time wondering how I would tell my family, how I would inform my friends. There was no way I was going to continue living in the closet when I knew how much better life would be when I could finally live as male.

Coming out was easy in some regards, and near impossible in others. My family was very accepting. I truly had no idea how they were going to react, so it was an immense relief when they welcomed me as their son, their grandson, their brother, their nephew. I'd never had a good relationship with my mother, but when I told her I was trans, she said, 'I know. I always knew.' And that was an amazing moment, because for the first time it felt like she understood me.

When I changed my name and started using male pronouns my relationships improved. I stopped acting out at home and refusing to leave the house because I was so anxious and depressed. I had the confidence to start socialising and spending time with family again. Life was looking up.

Some trans people's families aren't accepting at all. I can't imagine how difficult that must be, and I count myself extremely lucky for having such a supportive family. It's another reason that my personal experience of being trans has actually been quite positive. Being allowed to dress in masculine clothing at home and my parents using the right pronouns – all of this made me feel so much better. So much better that I'd truly plead with closeted trans people that you mustn't give up, no matter how hard it gets. Even if it seems like for ever, holding out for the time when you're free to present as your genuine self is so worth the wait.

The real problems arose when I wanted to come out at school. I asked for my year group to be informed of my new name and pronouns while I stayed at home for the day. Then I could come in the next day with everyone knowing the score. Of course, it wouldn't be easy, but I just wanted everyone to be informed of what was going on before I stepped into the lion's den.

My head teacher had other ideas. She said she simply couldn't inform the students without parental consent from every single student.

This was, of course, absurd. I don't need anyone's

permission to be my authentic self. I don't need signed approval on my identity from people who don't know anything about me – or from anyone at all, for that matter. Teachers and students get their names changed all the time and it's illegal in the UK to discriminate against people based on their sexuality and gender identity. But what followed was an uphill battle that lasted over a month, during which time I refused to go to school until my peers were informed I was transitioning.

Why was the topic of my transition so controversial? Why was my teacher so vehemently opposed to LGBTQIA+ children? These questions were never answered. I wonder if she knew how cruel and hurtful she was being. Or if she cared at all for my well-being, or that of the other trans kids who were going to go through our school system after me.

After a prolonged debate the issue was solved when the head teacher backed down. Just like that, she gave up. I'd missed all those weeks of school simply because my teacher was a bigot. She never apologised to me, or even explained her motives for denying my right to education. I was angry and hurt that I'd been treated as subhuman, but I had to get over it so I could continue at school.

However, this wasn't the only time I'd face discrimination in my school years. Teachers refused to use the right pronouns, and very few of my classmates used them either. Every morning the word 'female' was obnoxiously displayed next to my name on the classroom interactive whiteboard when my teacher took the register.

I wasn't allowed to use the male toilets (or the female; there were simply no toilets available to me apart from the disabled ones). Slurs were thrown at me wherever I went, mainly by students I didn't even know from other year groups. One boy told me that when he was being given a tour round the school someone pointed me out and said, 'And there's the tr***y.' Countless times I was harassed, bullied and mocked.

And yet, despite all of that, my school years weren't all bad.

While some people refused to respect my gender identity, others were extremely accepting. I played sports with the other boys. I spent every lunchtime with a group of my best friends, all cishet guys who did their level best to support me. Some of my teachers went out of their way to shut down transphobia, and, every year that went by, I felt more confident and secure in my male identity.

While I was completing my education, I was also trying to gain access to hormones. Due to various complications, waiting lists and plain bad luck, I wasn't able to get on testosterone until I left school. This was deeply distressing to me. While my friends were growing their first wispy little neckbeards, their voices cracking every five seconds, and shooting up in height, I was still short, squeaky and baby-faced. My dysphoria was at an all-time high, and with the pressure of exams and family issues, I became somewhat depressed.

Somehow I managed to salvage my grades. I was elated to be finished with school and moving on to bigger, better things. At this time I was sixteen years old. I was worried that I would be forced to start sixth form still not on hormones. I'd still be 'the trans kid'. I'd still stick out like a sore thumb among my six-foot-tall baritone buddies.

Summer had begun and it was time for prom. My mum bought me my first suit, which was a huge moment for me. I remember joking around with my dance teacher, a year or so before I'd come out as trans, promising her I wouldn't wear a dress to prom. 'You say that now,' she said, 'but in a few years you'll change your mind.'

I didn't.

As trans people, we often have these kinds of convictions that no one takes seriously. 'I will never wear a dress.' 'I hate sports.' 'I want to have short hair.' 'I don't want to wear make-up.' Other people dismiss it as a phase we're going through, that we'll someday grow out of. When we don't, we can look back and recognise these convictions as symptoms of our gender dysphoria.

Seeing myself in a suit felt incredible. I looked smart; I looked handsome. I took so many pictures of myself because it just felt so nice to approach this special occasion in the way that any other guy would. I was proud of myself for getting this far, and the boy I saw in the mirror was exactly who I wanted to be. I didn't think I could feel any more euphoric about my gender in one day.

When I arrived at prom, I took photos with all my friends so we could look back on the memories of that day. I could tell they were really pleased for me. We sat at the table together, which was great, not just because they were my friends, but because they accepted me as 'one of the guys'. I told them something that had been playing on my mind for a while. I joked around, saying I hoped I didn't get voted Prom Queen – except it wasn't a joke; I was genuinely worried about the prospect.

My buddies reassured me there was no way it would happen. But it really was the kind of cruel prank people might just play on me. I'd suffered through years of my peers invalidating my gender and making fun of me. I imagined the total silence and muffled laughter that would occur if my name was read out for Prom Queen. Kids are ruthless, and I wouldn't put it past them. It was a special kind of humiliation that I prayed no one had figured out would damage me more than anything.

Warily, I cast my vote and carried on eating. I was chatting with my friends, pretending everything was okay, all the while trying to calm my nerves. My stomach was churning. *Please don't say my name*, I thought. *Please*.

Words couldn't express my shock when my name was read out.

But not for the reason I'd feared.

My teachers and friends had conspired to vote me in for Prom King. They'd come through to respect my gender. They planned to make it happen because they knew how much it would mean to me – not the concept of being the most popular (I certainly wasn't), but the concept of earning that title.

It hadn't occurred to me that people might consider me the ideal candidate for Prom King. It hadn't occurred to me that I was worrying over nothing. It was engineered by my teachers and friends; their good deed for the day. It wouldn't make up for the snide comments some people had made and the way they had mocked me over the years. But those things no longer mattered – this was a sign that we'd all grown up. My classmates looked around and decided that being Prom King would be more special for me than anyone else in that room, and instead of voting for their friends or voting for the popular kids, they chose to give me that special moment.

Out of the hundred kids in our year group, I was walking up to the table to collect that sash and wear it with pride. I was so surprised, but so proud. I don't think I've ever experienced a more gender-euphoric moment: undeniably, indisputably, I was male. I didn't have to correct people; I didn't have to insist that I was just as much of a boy as anyone else. They did it for me. I was Prom King. The symbolism of that title, the purest form of gender validation... it's something I will treasure for the rest of my life.

After experiencing incredible moments like that, I worry that trans kids will be afraid that their lives will never be fulfilling or worthwhile. All of us are guilty of looking at others' post-op photos, telling ourselves, 'Not long now, and that will be me.' But why should we wait until we get surgery, hormones, name changes, whatever it may be to start living?

When I was younger, thinking about my future made me feel sad and uncertain. I looked at the women around me: my mother, my grandma, my teachers at school, people I walked by in the street. I couldn't see myself growing up to become them. I couldn't see myself having babies, wearing a wedding dress, wearing make-up.

I know that not wanting to do those things doesn't make me a man, because there are women who don't have kids, women who wear suits, and so on. But it went deeper than that. It went deeper than what clothes I wanted to wear and the choices I would make in life, in regard to having a family and getting married. It was a horrible sense of wrongness that influenced my entire childhood, and this pervading, hopeless idea that I would never get the chance to be happy. In my young mind, happiness was just a luxury I wasn't entitled to.

To cope, I turned to books. I spent all my time reading. In class, late at night in bed when I was supposed to be asleep, in the car, while I was walking. My mum ended up giving me all her YA vampire romance novels, so those were the worlds I was escaping to. Kid me thought *Twilight* was awesome.

This fixation on fiction is something a lot of trans people experience. I didn't want to engage with real life because it held nothing but disappointment for me. I just wanted to get lost in fantasy so I could forget who I was and live through the characters.

Then everything changed. Starting transition was the best decision I ever made, because it weaned me off escapism. I didn't have to engage in fantasy because real life wasn't so depressing any more. In fact, I've come to love my life.

Being named Prom King was the single most gender-euphoric moment I've experienced, but quite honestly, I feel gender euphoria every day.

Recently I've been thinking about what life would have been like if I hadn't transitioned. I wonder if I'd have been able to cope with living as a female, using female pronouns and hearing people use my birth name. I imagine how depressed and anxious I would feel; the way I'd keep myself to the confines of my bedroom and my books. I wonder if I would have forced myself to conform, to start wearing girls' clothes and make-up, just like everyone told me I would.

And after going down that rabbit hole, the what-ifs and the could-bes, I feel so, so grateful that I did come out as trans.

Sometimes I wake up and I can't help but smile when I see myself in the mirror. I'm not the self-conscious, bitter young girl who hid her body under baggy clothes, misbehaving at school and crying herself to sleep because she was so jealous of the boys in her class. I'm a proud and confident trans man, excited to go to university, excited to experience everything the world has to offer. I'm looking forward to the future and, whatever happens, I love and trust myself enough to get through it. I want my story to give people hope that being trans isn't a life sentence. I didn't need anyone's permission to be my authentic self, and neither do you.

Gender-Creative Parenting and Me

Halo Jedha Dawn

Queer non-binary writer, artist and parent based in London

I'm sitting in my study. It's another hot day, and outside my courgette leaves are turning crispy – I need to water them. I'm wearing linen shorts that nearly reach my knees. My legs are covered in a layer of fuzz, and a breeze curls pleasantly on the back of my neck. When I run my hand over my head, the short shave feels velvety under my fingers.

The house is quiet for once. Ember is thirteen months old and highly vocal; I'm used to hearing their fluent pre-verbal chatter, shouts of excitement and squawks of frustration. Today our friend Dot has taken Ember out in the sling for a walk to give them a nap. (Ember only naps while being held. I can't blame them.)

'I'm loving those shorts on you,' Dot said when they arrived. 'You're giving me soft-butch realness.' Yeah, I'm loving them too.

Normally helping Ember nap is my job. But right now my job is writing this essay. I feel free, self-expressive, and entirely ungendered. It hasn't always been this way.

*

Pregnancy, birth and breastfeeding are heavily gendered by society. It takes energy and creativity to experience them in a differently gendered way.

I felt it during pregnancy, fielding the inevitable question: 'Is it a boy or a girl?' Trying to find clothes that fitted over my bump, and despairing of floaty maternity clothes that clung to my curves. I wore square masculine garments, hippy pants, T-shirts and tatty waistcoats. I shaved the sides of my head and bleached what remained. The hard pink quiff did not flatter my oestrogen-softened face, but it was my rebellion against the ordained soft and feminine earth-mother role.

I felt it after the birth, in tough conversations with my partner about our careers. I wanted us to split work and childcare equally, but breastfeeding ate into my time – especially during three months of undiagnosed tongue-tie, resulting in endless feeds.

I'm not a woman, but I've lost income and career opportunities to feed my baby. I'm the one who's woken throughout the night, the one who can soothe them when no one else can. I've endured blistered nipples and countless teething bites. The experience of breastfeeding is anchored in womanhood. I'm not a woman, but I feel that anchor dragging on me.

We both took one month off work after the birth, and phased back gradually over the next four months. I had more freedom than Leo to take time off – partly thanks to statutory maternity allowance – but I was still determined to go back to part-time work as soon as possible. I'm self-employed, and work is essential for the health of my business, my creative fulfilment, gender expression and mental health. I've worked more than any of my female parent friends, and Leo has been a more active co-parent than any of their partners. But after a few months I was still chafing against the imbalance: Leo working four and a half days and me two or three days every week, which we achieved through working Saturdays, and using one or two days of paid childcare.

I agreed to the compromise, but it still rubbed on me like a scratchy clothing label. My work was interrupted by near-constant breastfeeds. I was jealous of Leo's freedom to focus on their projects. Why should my career take second place?

We're both non-binary. Neither of us are 'mum' or 'dad'. In dominant culture the words are loaded with gendered meaning and unwelcome expectations. In so many cases *Dad* is absent, the breadwinner, only around at weekends, barely finishing work in time for bedtime. *Mum* is a martyr, sacrificing work, hobbies and personal satisfaction to the full-time job of childcare and housekeeping. Both roles are alienating, unfulfilling and unfair.

'What will your child call you?' people asked us, and our first answer was, 'Well, it's up to them.' Ember will decide what to call us in time. But meanwhile, we've chosen ungendered nicknames for ourselves: Leo is Zaza, and I'm Boo.

Boo: partly for Big Boo from *Orange is the New*

Black, a soft-butch-queer-daddy icon, but mostly short for Boob Parent.

My boobs filled out. They became round and rock-hard; milk leaked everywhere. I wore bras for the first time in two decades, just to have somewhere to stick the breast pads. All the nursing tops were painfully feminine. I wore men's T-shirts, shoving them up under my armpit when it was time to feed. I tried collared shirts and waistcoats but, breastfeeding every hour or so, I couldn't be bothered with the buttons.

When Ember was six weeks old, one of my oldest friends got married. Somehow we got there through seemingly non-stop feeds, vomiting and nappy changes. It was a bakingly hot August day, it was a queer wedding and I was determined to dress up. I wore a blue three-piece trouser suit with a flamboyant pink-and-blue shirt and a magenta tie. Purple eyebrows, fresh pink hair dye and glitter eyeshadow completed the look. I was the most stylish bisexual dandy to ever breastfeed in a church.

Leo and Ember wore matching skirt and waistcoat outfits: I found an adorable babygro printed with a waistcoat, shirt and bow tie. As I drove I caught sight of my reflection in the rear-view mirror and felt a glow of pride. I looked glam rock as fuck. 'I feel like I'm *doing* my gender for the first time in months,' I told Leo. 'It feels good.'

At the wedding I unbuttoned my shirt, pushed my tie aside and breastfed in my suit. The crowd was daringly and gorgeously queer: one groom in a regal silk skirt suit with a tailcoat and bustle, the other in a pastel-pink dinner jacket, their best person a trans woman. I beamed at everyone, soaking up the vibes.

It's been a pleasure to create our own roles as Zaza and Boo. Leo has mobility issues, which means they can't carry Ember around, so Zaza's role has so far mostly been a seated one: books, toys, snacks and stories, plus whatever housework tasks they can. I do breastfeeding, bed-sharing, slinging, nap walks, tidying, hoovering, the dishwasher and gardening. We take turns to cook. I don't get as much playtime with Ember because I'm often doing the chores Leo can't do.

When Covid-19 came along and all our childcare was cancelled, it shook up our work arrangements for the better. Leo and I split childcare evenly during lockdown. *Everyone's* work was compromised. We settled into a new rhythm: each of us working an hour here, an hour there. The emergency freed Leo of the pressure to work full time – and me from that nagging sense of unfairness.

Ember spends a lot of time on my body. I do housework with them in the sling, and as lockdown dragged on I shouldered more of the physical work. The genderedness of the experience resonated through my bones. How many billions of women have worn their babies on their backs while cooking meals, hanging nappies and digging earth? I simultaneously felt solidarity with other baby-wearing, breastfeeding parents through the ages, and deeply uncomfortable to be forced into such a feminised role.

I read infuriating reports of incompetent, self-centred husbands on feminist Twitter: women juggling the lion's share of housework and childcare during lockdown alongside full-time jobs. I refused to be one of them. Simply claiming non-binary identity isn't enough to opt out of sex-based oppression – we also have to radically shift the patterns of our lives.

But despite the miasma of sexism that clings to housework like the bad smell around our unemptied food-composting bin, gender expectations are *not* why I clean more than Leo. I'm simply the able-bodied one. As I struggled with this I realised I had no models of domestic labour that weren't feminine. But why shouldn't housework be masculine? What could be more rugged and dad-ly than being strong and active, busting around looking after everyone's physical needs? It certainly keeps me fit – I'm more hench than I've ever been.

Gender is a figment of consciousness, and I'm free to conceive of my role however I want.

Our mums were socialised to prioritise the needs of others over their own. But at other times and in other places, service has been gendered masculine. What if instead of feeling like an overworked mum, I thought of myself as a butler or valet? A gentleman's gentleman? A houseboy?

Is gender inherent in our division of labour – or am I misgendering us both by viewing things through the lens of male and female roles?

Helping the people I love and making their lives better is a pleasure. Why should caring for our habitat be a woman thing? I'm an action queer, a service enby.[*]

All I needed was a shift in consciousness.

Well, almost. I also needed to give my aching muscles a rest and take off the sling. Now Leo does childcare while I clean and tidy: we're both doing feminised work. I'm less tired – and I don't have to keep tiny reaching hands out of the knife drawer.

Kate Bornstein's pioneering 1994 book *Gender Outlaw* breaks our experience of gender down into component parts. There are gender roles (the gendered social roles we perform), gender assignation (the gender people assume we are), gender expression (how we present through our clothing, hair, manner, body language and speech) and gender identity (how we feel inside). Pregnancy and parenting has shown me how uncomfortable it can be when these clash with each other. Bringing my gender expression into alignment was the next step.

My short hair grew out. When it was unbearably shaggy I asked Leo to clipper it. Deep down I wanted to shave it off completely – various cis friends had gone for the lockdown buzzcut; it was practically acceptable. But I didn't dare. I was scared that I'd be ugly without hair. Three decades of conditioning to be 'pretty' were too hard to overcome.

---

[*] Enby = NB = non-binary.

Instead Leo shaved everything except the front. From the back, a buzzcut; from the front, a floppy side fringe. When I saw myself in the mirror I liked my reflection; and I liked feeling the air on the back of my neck. It was half masc and half femme, a Halo original.

As lockdown eased I went to a socially distanced picnic and couldn't find any hot-weather clothes I felt comfortable in. I ended up borrowing things off Leo, and once we were home, I hit the online sales.

What was my summer style? Femme clothes put me on edge, but straight masculinity didn't appeal. We have so few representations of androgyny in our culture, and they're all white and skinny, or villainous and unattractive. Where are my curvy, size Large, non-binary role models?

Inspired by *Queer Eye*, I looked for short-sleeved cotton shirts with bold prints of birds and leaves. Linen shorts with deep pockets. Men's-cut vest tops. I'd avoided the latter, thinking the high necklines weren't suitable for breastfeeding, but fuck it, I'd just cut the armpits bigger and go in from the side.

As my dysphoria surged I booked a session with my therapist. I talked about feeling trapped, about my struggle to do rewarding work and express my gender around breastfeeding.

There was nothing to be done about the pandemic and my partner's disability. But with pregnancy and parenting, I started to confront the fact that *I* had made choices that constrained me.

I chose to conceive and gestate Ember rather than adopt or use a surrogate. I chose to do extended breastfeeding even though it meant I couldn't start testosterone. I made those choices for good reasons: curiosity, pride and Ember's well-being. It's on me to own them.

'You're exhausted,' my therapist said. 'Can you take half an hour for self-care? Have a nap, a shower, whatever you want?'

I knew what I wanted.

In the bathroom my reflection stared back. Why was this hard? Was I really so invested in whether I was attractive to cis men? Was I so afraid to find out what my face looked like?

I put the size-two guard on the clippers, took a breath, and started at the front. It only took a moment to shave it off.

The result was startling. Most startling of all was that I *liked* it. More than how it looked, I liked how it *felt*. I liked how it felt to shrug off three decades of socialisation. I liked how it felt to opt out of the pressure to be pretty. My shaved head looked hard, no-nonsense. It looked like someone who didn't give a fuck how they looked. It looked like it would feel nice to touch.

As I stepped out of the bathroom I felt lighter. No more measuring myself against beauty standards I was never going to meet. No more masking my transness under a deniable layer of femininity. I was out and proud.

Testosterone is off the table for now – but there are

other ways to queer my presentation. I'm planning tattoo sleeves emphasising my baby-boosted biceps. With inked arms and a shaved head I'll give off strong butch vibes.

As I got used to my new hair I discovered I liked my face. I can see the clean lines of my head. I thought my features would seem heavy and blocky without hair, but they just look – well, human. My face and nose are balanced and symmetrical. And are those cheekbones?

There's a radical self-acceptance in seeing myself without decoration. This is me. This is what I look like.

I like it.

I like being able to rinse my head under the tap on a hot day. I like not worrying about my hair getting greasy. I like not needing shampoo or styling products. It's breezy and quick and practical. And it looks fucking boss.

Ember is feeding less during the day now. I've stopped wearing nursing bras. When I do feed, my 'menswear' is more convenient than I had expected. A loose tank top, a short-sleeved cotton shirt over that. It takes a moment to unbutton the shirt and pull the vest down.

I feel so much more comfortable. Is it just gender euphoria, or is menswear better made than womenswear? The shorts are lined, tailored, with deep pockets. They don't cling, don't dig in at the waist. The fabric is breathable. I can squat, sit down, bend over. In these clothes I'm not conscious of my boobs or stomach. I feel relaxed in myself. I feel just the right size.

Leo and I knew, without discussing it, that we wouldn't

force our child into the gender binary. We both know how traumatic it can be – why would we assign a gender at birth?

It was scary, crafting the email to family explaining that we were using they/them pronouns for Ember; raising them not as a 'boy' or 'girl', but in an empowering environment free of gendered expectations. Some of our relatives accepted it, and some pushed back.

At first I struggled with the inevitable 'boy or girl?' question from new acquaintances. But the more I practised the easier it got. I usually say something like, 'They're too young for that sort of thing – we're leaving gender until they're old enough to tell us what they want to be.'

Mostly I get confused acceptance. Sometimes people insist on gendering Ember – I usually smile and ignore it. If we have an important relationship we'll have the conversation, as many times as it takes.

Even if they get the pronouns wrong, people often respond positively. Some say, 'What a great idea – it makes total sense.' I once heard, 'Yes, a lot of people are doing that now,' (are they?) and one old lady said, 'Quite right, they all choose their own way.'

I don't mind how strangers gender Ember – but by explaining our choices, perhaps we're injecting the possibility of gender freedom into their world.

At this age, gender-creative parenting means not worrying about what's for 'boys' and what's for 'girls'. It means being careful in our language, praising their smiles and helpfulness as well as their strength and boldness. I try not to comment on their appearance too much, although it's hard when they're so darn cute.

We dress them for comfort: leggings, T-shirts, hoodies with animal ears, dresses and patterned shorts. Their wardrobe is green, orange, yellow, red, purple, blue and pink. Their toy box contains blocks and stackers, soft animals, shape-sorters, trucks and diggers. Contrary to what the clothing stores suggest, gender-neutral isn't white and grey – it's about embracing the rainbow.

We'll let them choose their clothes as soon as they can. If they want to leave the house in a tutu, odd shoes and a Batman T-shirt, all power to them.

Ember loves books. I've curated their collection to avoid harmful gender ideas. It's been fun finding inclusive and queer-friendly titles. We love: *A is for Activist*, a rousing alphabet book in which F is for feminist, L is for LGBT and T is for trans; *Julián Is a Mermaid*, in which a young boy dreams of being a beautiful mermaid and receives support from an unexpected quarter; *Knights and Dragons, Unite!*, in which peace-loving enemies team up to end their conflict with a talent show (so wholesome, so gay); and *The Paper Bag Princess*, in which the princess outwits the dragon, rescues the prince, and refuses to marry him when he turns out to be a sexist snob.

My favourite books of all tackle sexual reproduction and the gender binary head on. I bought them for Ember, but it turns out I needed them too.

There's *What Makes a Baby* by Cory Silverberg, which explains human reproduction without mentioning sex or gender once. It's suitable for every kind of family, and fits IVF and surrogacy as well as adoption and caesarean birth. It's the perfect antidote to the misgendering I received throughout my pregnancy. Each time we read it I retell the story of Ember's conception, gestation and birth in a way that respects my gender. I feel a weight lifting from me; I finally feel like I fit.

Then there's *Alien Nation* by Matty Donaldson. When I first read it I cried.

When baby aliens are born they're sent to Planet Girl or Planet Boy, based on whether they're closer to pink or blue – even if they're orange, purple or green. The planets have strict rules about how to behave. Seeing the gender binary described like that I felt a fresh round of grief about the needless violence of it.

Eventually the aliens rip up the rules, build a bridge between the planets and create a brand-new planet for the aliens who don't fit. It was immensely, unexpectedly healing for me to see non-binary experience clearly explained in a children's book. 'Some of the aliens weren't comfortable being on either planet' – *wow!* It's not just me? That feeling is normal, and valid – and ultimately leads to more freedom and choice for everyone? The cheerful pictures and simple language were validating at a deep emotional level. I felt seen and celebrated.

We're creating choice, not imposing non-binary gender. We aren't assigning *any* gender – including a non-binary one. If Ember wants feminine things or masculine things they can have them, from toys and clothes to names and pronouns. If they claim some neo-gender we've never heard of, we'll thank them for expanding our horizons. If they change their mind every week, we'll embrace the fluidity.

Our aim is to raise a child without gender trauma. We won't be able to protect them from the wider world, and gender violence is everywhere. But by listening to them and respecting them we're hoping to build their resilience and trust in us so that we can support them through whatever they face.

By not assigning a gender we're not only disrupting the male/female binary, we're disrupting the trans/cis binary. If trans is not being the gender you were assigned at birth, and cis is being the gender you were assigned at birth, by our current definitions Ember won't be trans *or* cis. It feels healing and radical to change the rules of the game. I look forward to learning what Ember's generation has to teach us about gender.

My first step towards gender liberation was to cherry-pick expressions and roles from the available menu and build a non-binary identity for myself that feels like the best of both worlds. I am – or strive to be – strong, nurturing, protective, gentle, ambitious, artistic and direct. I'm emotionally available and in touch with my vulnerability. I'm a proud business owner and provider for my family. When I embrace masculinity, I feel liberated to vibe with femininity in a more consensual, intentional way.

But all of us have been coerced into masculinity or femininity, and all of us have gender trauma. I have ex-boyfriends who pressured me to be submissive and feminine, to wear long hair and pretty clothes. They preyed on my vulnerability and undermined my confidence.

My second step towards gender liberation has been realising that femininity and masculinity are both traumatic, both irredeemably toxic. My trauma doesn't undermine my transness: it's a symptom of a broken system, a sign of how much we need new stories and new ways of experiencing ourselves.

We are all traumatised and we all need healing. For me, gender freedom is more than mixing and matching from the binary – it's throwing off those shackles entirely, and helping raise a generation who frame bodies, self-expression and social dynamics in an entirely new way.

Sometimes gender healing is sorting out the division of labour in your household – or changing the way you relate to it. Sometimes it's writing a chapter about gender that forces you to confront your dysphoria and change your clothes and hair. And sometimes it's parenting in a way that heals gender trauma rather than perpetuating it.

When we raise our children free to do their gender however they want, it's healing for us, too.

The First Signs Hormones Were Working for Me

Laura Kate Dale

Twenty-nine, autistic trans woman and full-time author, living near London

When I think back to my first few months on hormone replacement therapy, a lot of my memories are of me questioning whether I was experiencing actual changes to my mind and body, or seeing changes that didn't yet exist out of a mixture of excitement and eagerness. I think it's pretty easy to understand why: starting on hormones was for a long time the finish line in a road of medical-system hurdles being placed between me and the body I one day hoped to have.

My road to getting prescribed oestrogen on the NHS in the UK took a lot longer for me than it was ever really meant to. The NHS system for arranging treatment for trans people is a slow and methodical process when it's working as intended, and any delays to that system tend to add up quickly. On a good day you're waiting between six and twelve months per appointment, and longer for your initial consultation, with multiple different doctors at different appointments having to sign off in agreement before you can proceed. Throw on top of that the fact that I experienced a year-long delay when my initial referral was lost, multiple issues where appointment letters were received after appointments were due to have occurred, and as a result I spent many years bouncing around the system trying to get help.

It took several years for me to eventually get on hormones, and I was painfully aware of all the time spent waiting.

While I was waiting to start hormones, my body was still undergoing some of the changes of my initial testosterone-based puberty. I was watching my hairline beginning to recede, my facial and body hair getting thicker, and noticing my build continuing to change in size and shape. Every day I had testosterone running through me, I knew my body would become more masculine, and those masculinising changes would be more difficult to reverse in the years to come. I didn't like what my body was becoming, and starting hormones was the light at the end of the tunnel keeping me going. It was the hope I held on to, the emergency exit from a puberty I could not halt alone.

So, like many people who eventually start hormone replacement therapy after a lengthy wait, I started looking for signs that it was working from day one. I'm aware most of the signs I spotted early on were mostly in my head, but that didn't make them any less important in the weeks and months after I started on hormones.

Firstly, there was the overwhelming sense of calm and

relief I felt almost immediately after starting HRT. This was likely nothing to do with the oestrogen itself, and everything to do with the knowledge that I was taking the oestrogen. It would be easy to label that a placebo effect, but I think it's a little more nuanced than that. I had started hormones, which meant that, to a greater or lesser degree, my body would soon start to change. At the very least, the changes I was uncomfortable with would start to slow down. At best, I would eventually start to see changes going in the other direction, bringing my body more in line with what I wanted it to be. Sure, the hormones themselves were probably not changing my mood chemically yet, but the knowledge that my body was on the road to pulling a U-turn hormonally was enough to make me feel so much better in myself.

Then came some of the first actual emotional changes, which were much more obviously a result of the oestrogen. The first time I noticed them was when, a few months into taking the pills, I went to see a film at the cinema and cried for a solid five minutes at a slightly emotional advert for a car. The specifics of the advert were pretty tacky in hindsight, something about a parent using the car to make it to their kid's performance at school on time, but it just hit me in a way I hadn't expected. It was cynical advertising, but it hit me hard emotionally.

Over the weeks that followed, I discovered this was no mere fluke. I was suddenly becoming vulnerable to cynical emotional pulls in advertising, which was certainly not something I had particularly experienced before.

While it was initially a little intense, I was ultimately really happy with the changes I was experiencing to my emotional range. I was feeling my feelings much more richly and deeply than before, and seemed to be able to better verbalise the nuances of how I was feeling day to day.

Changes to my body were what I was most eager to see happen, and also the hardest aspect of my transition to notice in the short term. I can today look back on pictures of myself a decade ago and see how my face shape has changed, my body fat has redistributed to give me more of an appearance of hips, and how much my chest has developed. But, as with any hormone-based puberty, the changes come slowly, and may be hard to notice in real time.

There are a lot of little physical changes that happened over those first few months, which were small enough to be written off as psychosomatic. I noticed a diminished muscle mass, lessened physical strength, and some pretty noticeable differences to my tolerance for extremes of temperature. I grew up fairly immune to temperature conditions; I'd happily wear heavy jackets in the summer and shorts in the winter without batting an eye. But within a few weeks of starting on HRT I was finding myself a lot more at the whims of the weather. I needed a heavy-duty fan in the summer, blankets in the winter, and was much more physically aware of my body's relationship to the temperature around me.

While I spent months and months watching for any visible tiny changes in my body, the first moment I remember really being aware my body was changing actually completely snuck up on me out of the blue. It was a moment of pure gender euphoria: the first time I felt my breasts bounce.

To set the scene a little, at this point in my transition I didn't really have any breasts to speak of, at least as far as I could see them, looking down from above. I would usually wear stuffed bras with outfits, just to give my clothing some shape and hopefully lead to me being gendered correctly more frequently by strangers. There wasn't enough breast tissue to require support, and I had just sort of assumed that nothing was happening yet in that regard. Bras were more aesthetic in outfits rather than functional. They existed to signal I was female to strangers, and to help me feel more safe accessing gendered spaces without fear my presence would be questioned.

I had noticed some pain in my chest a few weeks into HRT, and some noticeable tenderness in my nipples, but I hadn't really thought much of it. Maybe there was some explanation for that other than breast-tissue development; I didn't want to get my hopes up until there was some tangible evidence I could see. Granted, looking down from above is the worst way to get a proper sense of breast development, but I didn't know that at the time.

The day itself was really normal. I was busy working up in my office, the workaholic that I've always been, writing with a looming deadline. I decided to sprint downstairs quickly to grab some food, which I would take back to the office to eat. That was when I noticed, with each step down the stairs I took, I could feel my breasts bounce. A physical sensation that resonated in my chest, and instantly left me ecstatic.

While I couldn't really see that much had outwardly changed, that moment felt like my body raising its voice to me, telling me not to worry, changes were coming. Even if I couldn't see the difference, things were changing. It was a new physical sensation, tied to breast development, and even if I couldn't see it, I could feel it, which, if anything, was more affirming to me at that moment.

I'm not ashamed to say that I found as many excuses as possible for the rest of the day to walk back and forth up and down stairs. It became my pick-me-up when I felt like the changes my body was undergoing were not happening as fast as I hoped. It was my reassurance that I was undoing the damage testosterone had done, little by little. I wasn't imagining it: my body was changing, and I was so happy.

The happiness I felt at knowing I was really undergoing second puberty was all-encompassing, and in stark contrast to how I felt in my teens, when puberty first became a part of my life. Where the first time I had found every change to feel alien and uncomfortable, oestrogen puberty's changes were actively exciting. That served as a really reassuring early sign that HRT was the correct choice for me. It told me that puberty was going to be different this time, a wonderful period of self-discovery rather than a period of trying to ignore the existence of my own body as best I could.

Breast development on HRT for trans women like myself, who first underwent testosterone puberty, is a bit of a gamble at the best of times. Statistically, most of us end up developing breasts at least a few cup sizes below those of our family averages, and for most an A cup is the likely end result. I know that without undergoing surgery I'm likely to never have a particularly notable set of breasts, but feeling them bounce when I run or go up and down stairs was a big part of me coming to love my breasts exactly the way they are. It's a reminder they exist. They're mine. They're a part of my body, a part I grew, and a part of my body that won't ever go away.

Puberty takes a long time, and that's easy to forget. My initial testosterone puberty dragged out over years, and I know it was a little foolish of me to assume that my second puberty would for some reason be much faster. I knew it was going to be years before things really changed for me, but I was still incredibly thankful for some sign to hold on to, something that let me know that journey had begun, and even if it was going to take years, it was going to be okay now.

I might have still had broad shoulders, my facial hair wouldn't go away, I couldn't buy shoes in my size, and clothes didn't fit my arm length very well, but that little bit of bounce on my upper torso told me I was changing and growing. It's such a small thing, but it's a regular source of euphoria that, even years later, I make sure not to take for granted. A little daily joy, and reminder that my body is no longer the one it once was.

My Mr's Mr: Ensuring I Got a Gender-Affirming Wedding

Miles Nelson

Autistic author and trans man living in Durham,
UK, who came out at age seventeen

I'm about to tell you a story that began six and a half years ago. When a boy met a 'girl', who turned out to be a boy as well.

That 'girl' was me, and that boy's name was Chris. We first met through *Pokémon X and Y*, a week after its release. We'd play together whenever we had a break from studying. A month later we met for the first time outside of sixth form for our first *Pokémon* tournament, ready and willing to face each other and duke it out for the crown. There he asked me out by nicknaming his team of six creatures to spell out a romantic message. We both lost the tournament, but took home something far, far more important.

Around two years later I came out as a trans man and began my social transition. Looking back, I did not handle my coming out well. Many people were shocked when I posted it online, even those I thought already knew.

Moreover, many were angry they hadn't been told first.

All in all, it was a mess. Through it all, though, Chris stood by me, faithful and supportive. He was my rock through those dark times.

Three years after my social transition began, on our fifth anniversary, he went down on one knee and proposed by placing the ring on the wrong finger.

Despite all our mistakes and trepidation leading up to this moment, it was perfect. All three sets of parents were overjoyed. Everyone exchanged their coos and awws.

I had planned to start medically transitioning before our wedding. I wanted our wedding day to be a day that I could feel completely and undeniably like *me*. I had dreamed of walking down the aisle and becoming my Mr's Mr, and of it being *my* ceremony and not the ceremony of someone who no longer exists. Sadly, that could not be the case. Despite long-standing pleas to doctors, there was extraordinarily little I could do to speed up the process. It took an appointment of two minutes for a referral to go through, thanks to a single fantastic doctor, and even then, I knew it might be years before I could start therapy.

It was also during this process that I began to wonder if HRT was really the right path for me; after all, in all physical aspects, except for my voice, I could pass for male. And having struggled before with hormonal birth control, I was hesitant to plunge my body into yet more disarray.

More than anything, though, Chris and I wanted to take this opportunity to celebrate just how far we'd come.

It was around this time my partner and I, by complete chance, attended an appointment for a late-availability offer at our dream wedding venue. It was a beautiful, traditional room in an old farmhouse, its walls covered in flowers and mosses trailing from wooden rafters. It had a separate bar, perfect for a quiet moment away from the lights and music for those who needed it.

We booked our wedding then and there.

There were four months between the date we made the reservation and our big day, on 15 December 2019. Looking back, we were luckier than we could ever have known.

Soon after came the first inkling that things might not be so easy as they seemed. Eighteen years ago, my parents divorced, and it was an unpleasant affair. This would be their first time standing in the same room since the court hearings battling for custody over me.

Our invitations brought to light skeletons in people's closets, and ugly feelings that had long been buried.

There were, in particular, my father's parents. Within our family they are respected, and dare I say, slightly feared. Stoic and tough, businesslike and proud... their legacy was a defining factor of the generation before mine.

My husband-to-be was always under their scrutiny. In their eyes, he was the 'man of the house', and they certainly didn't know that our house had two. For a long time my grandparents were the only people who didn't know about my identity. At some point they simply seemed to get left behind. As the years passed us by, my visits to them grew fewer, and ever more intimidating to me. They still didn't know about my husband's many tattoos, so how could I possibly tell them about this?

I have the feeling that they had suspected something for a long, long time, though; it wasn't easy to miss the Mr & Mr Valentine's cards on our hearth, or the giant trans flag on the wall. Even so, every passing Christmas seemed to bring make-up and ladies' socks.

But as my other grandparents gave me grandson cards and tried their hardest to embrace my name, I found it harder and harder to face my paternal grandparents, even as the chance to talk slipped steadily away.

We couldn't send an invite without them seeing the note we'd written to our guests.

There will be no bride at this wedding. We ask that all guests respect this by using the correct pronouns and name. We're not asking you to accept this, but please respect it so that we can enjoy our perfect day to the fullest.

There was no hiding it any more.

One day, as summer waned and the leaves began to fall, I made the decision to visit them alone and sort things out face to face.

I walked into their quiet, old-English styled home, trying not to look as terrified as I felt. They greeted me warmly, tea was made, and chocolate biscuits served on a pretty floral platter.

'I've brought you an invitation to our wedding,' I said.

My grandparents exchanged a glance.

'But I want to talk about something first.'

So we talked. For close to an hour we spoke of what they knew and had suspected. I talked about my identity, and what it meant for them. I was becoming a man and marrying one too.

'Why would you want to be a man if you're marrying one anyway?'

'Well... I've always been attracted to both, so it's not much of a change for me. Even if I hadn't met Chris, I might have ended up marrying a woman anyway.'

'Is that even legal?'

'It has been for... five years or so, now.'

'But you can't be a man. Not physically... right?'

'The procedures do exist. One day I might grow a beard and drop my voice. But we'll see.'

The conversation continued, tense at times, but never unpleasant. We talked about my future and the wedding, until I finally finished my tea. Then I drove home, feeling unburdened and a little bit faint.

When I got home, my phone rang. It was my dad's voice, and the first thing he said was, 'Your grandad called.'

My blood ran cold. 'Yeah?'

'Yeah. You've got bigger balls than I ever did.'

I laughed, heart pounding even as my eyes welled up with tears. 'Were they mad?' I asked.

'No,' he said. 'They were shocked, but they'll get over it.'

'Good.'

'I'm proud of you.'

In the end, my grandparents did not come to our wedding. But they were very clear it was no fault of mine. The bitter rift between my two families ran deeper than I had ever known, but my grandparents respected me for what I told them, even if they didn't necessarily show it.

Soon after, we had our appointment at the local registry office to make our date official. By then it was three months until our wedding, and little time to spare.

We sat down before being taken to individual interviews. After that we were brought together once more. The three of us talked, and we signed our contracts, as the registrar explained the process and the ceremony.

She placed a different form in front of each of us.

I looked down at mine, then glanced across at his.

Our forms were different. He filled in the form to become my husband, whereas I filled in the one to be his wife. I knew it had to be done, but even so, my hand shook as I held the pen. I wrote down the name that I had been born with, my birth sex, and ticked the title of 'Mrs'. Did I want my father to walk me down the aisle, giving me away to my future husband? No. Of course not.

I looked up as she began to speak.

'Do you two have any questions?'

I swallowed, nodding. 'When we declare our names,' I began, 'what if I have another name I prefer?'

'You can answer as quietly as you wish,' she reassured.

'Then we can use your preferred name for the rest of the ceremony. Anything else?'

I took a deep breath.

'I'm trans. Is... there any way I could change the wording a little in the verbal contract?' I asked. 'Because I... I'm not going to be his wife.'

She froze, glancing from me to my husband and back again. 'The words have to be said exactly as they appear. You must declare him your husband, and he must declare you his wife.'

I thought I was prepared for this moment, but somehow I wasn't. I bent my head as tears streamed down my cheeks. 'We can't say that... not in front of everyone.'

'Are you on hormones? Perhaps if you could get a note from your doctor—'

I shook my head. 'I'm not. Not yet, at least.'

She hesitated. I felt Chris wrap his arm around my shoulders.

'Is there any other way?' he asked. I was grateful, as the words somehow kept escaping me.

'Well, we... perhaps we can work around it. What are you afraid of?'

'I... I just...' I took a breath, shaking my head in an effort to regain composure. 'I've fought so hard to become the man I am now. But some of the people there... some of them still don't see it. And for the ones that do...' I trailed off.

'It's okay. I understand.'

'I... I could do it, but not in front of the guests.'

She nodded. 'All the marriage needs to be legal is your two witnesses. We can escort you from the room and perform your legal vows alone. How would you feel about that?'

'Will anyone notice?'

'Not a soul. It will be just like any other ceremony.'

My fiancé looked at me. I could see in his eyes he was asking if it was enough.

Finally I nodded. 'That'll work.'

The rest of our appointment passed in something of a haze. After that moment I didn't remember much.

A little under half an hour later we headed home. I drove in silence for a few minutes before I finally heard Chris speak.

'Are you okay?'

I roused myself, blinking, and glanced towards him. 'Yes, of course.'

'Are you sure?'

I glanced back to the road, ticked on the indicator and turned the steering wheel. 'I thought I was prepared. It's as though the realisation flipped a switch in me. But I'm fine now.'

'What about the compromise?'

I nodded. 'It hurts that you, of all people, have to call me... that. But I'm happy, so long as we're the only ones who'll ever know.'

He nodded.

'Well, us and our witnesses.'

I smiled. 'Yeah.'

Now might be a good time to mention that my husband and I had a 'best dude' each: Taylor (they/them) and Alan (he/him). The two of them have been with us from the very beginning of our relationship, and my transition. We were more than excited to share our day with them.

The two of them were honoured to be part of our wedding. Even more than that, I knew that they'd be understanding of the situation at hand.

They arranged our joint stag do, in which we went axe-throwing. I enjoyed myself hugely despite only landing a single throw; Chris, on the other hand, landed almost every single shot. Taylor was amused. Alan was baffled. Not even he, who went throwing on a regular basis, hit as many. Meanwhile I settled for being slightly scared.

We left the centre laughing and joking, went for a few drinks in a quiet bar and reminisced about our years together. We clinked glasses, both alcoholic and non, and grinned.

Autumn soon became winter, and Christmas decorations went up. Our nerves heightened and Christmas meals were filled with a different sort of excited buzz. Everyone wanted to know our plans down to the tiniest details. My soon-to-be mother-in-law bought an entire supermarket's supply of butter to ice our wedding cake.

My mum's tailor-made outfit finally arrived. Everyone else had rainbow socks.

I got the wrong shirt tailored and had to hope no one would notice it was slightly too long on the arms. In all fairness, I'm quite glad I now have a tailored shirt to wear to casual events.

Before we knew it, the day had come. We rode to our venue in a camper van twinkling with congratulations, a bottle of champagne in the drinks cooler. We loaded it up with dozens of rainbow favours, board-book copies of the LGBTQIA+ children's book *And Tango Makes Three* for our youngest guests, and rainbow flags to decorate.

Despite never feeling carsick in my life, the journey was nauseating. What if something went wrong? What if the car broke down? What if the registrars forgot our wishes, and embarrassed us in front of our three families?

It was almost too much to bear, and with five hours to go when we arrived, it felt at first like the longest day of my life.

We spent time with family opening cards and gifts before returning to our room. We got changed in separate rooms of our honeymoon suite, only for our best men to surprise us while we were still in our underwear.

Finally we were ready. The door was opened and we beheld our waiting grooms.

It was hard to keep back the tears. His suit was bright silver, with a pink shirt underneath. Mine was striped purple, and I wore with it a blue shirt.

Between us we had only our rainbow lapel flowers in common.

I felt sexier in that suit than I ever had before. I felt certain that no one, even myself, would be able to picture me any other way.

Teary-eyed, we took one another's hands and pulled each other into a loving hug and a kiss. 'Hey, handsome,' he said.

'You look amazing.'

We gave each other one last smile, adjusted one another's ties and collars. Soon after we walked hand in hand to the bar where guests were beginning to gather.

I stepped into that room as the man I was born to be.

Taylor and Alan were doing their best to greet the guests, and we took that moment to engage our photographer for our first photo shoot together. Drinks were offered. Soon we were called into our ceremony room. Our officiants were two of our county's most senior registrars, and they spoke with understanding and kindness that began to ease my nerves immediately. It was our first time meeting them, but they carried all the notes from our first appointment. They handled the situation with all the delicacy of people who had been overseeing weddings longer than we had been alive.

We left feeling reassured, our excitement renewed.

Finally, just under a hundred guests began to take their seats, leaving my husband and I alone at the bar. The world was silent as we took deep breaths and exchanged nervous glances. The bartender offered us a beer each, which we gratefully accepted.

Then our song began to play.

We exchanged a last glance, squeezed one another's hands, and began our walk down the aisle. We reached the front, still gripping each other's hands, not knowing what else to do. The registrars smiled. 'It's now we'd tell you two to hold hands, but it looks like that's already covered.'

Everyone laughed.

And with that, the ceremony began.

We stuttered our vows through sheets of tears, and for the first time I didn't feel like less of a man for crying. Luckily, we weren't the only ones; there wasn't a dry eye in the room. It was an awkward affair, all things considered, but a lot of people afterwards said that it was the most beautiful wedding they'd ever seen.

Chris's vows told a story of learning what love truly is. How it transcends gender, transcends sexuality, and how love without limits is the truest love of all.

I told of how, of all the stories I'd written, ours was the most fantastical of them all. I vowed to be there for him until the very end. Oh, and I managed to sneak a *Pokémon* pun or two in there as well.

And finally, the ceremony came to an end.

'With all that said, I can now pronounce you two life partners,' the officiant said, and we formalised the sentiment with a tearful kiss.

Shortly after, we left the room and made our marriage official under the gaze of our witnesses. A single moment and it was over, and Chris hadn't even let go of my hand.

Our waiting guests were none the wiser.

The rest of the night passed in a blur.

Funnily enough, one of the most mundane events of the night stuck with me the most.

It happened when I visited the bathroom to clear my

senses. While I was washing my hands, a relative of ours walked in. During planning, we had discovered his history of transphobia, and I couldn't help being anxious. We'd fretted a lot about the invitation and the things he might say on our day.

Of all the places to run into one another, it just had to be in the men's bathroom, didn't it?

His brows rose a little, but to my surprise, he smiled.

Stunned, all I could say was, 'Hey.'

'How's your night?' he asked.

I could only grin stupidly as I answered, 'Amazing.'

We had a short conversation after that, but I was eager to get back to the festivities, and my groom. In the end, he simply shook my hand and wished me warm congratulations.

Not even our sweetheart table collapsing or a stray glass of orange juice in the corner of our family photos could dampen our spirits.

After a long night of laughing, dancing and drinking, the celebration finally ended. My husband and I returned to our room hand in hand, slightly tipsy but hearts full of joy.

We made good use of the hot tub despite the mid-December breeze and the faint twinkling of frost across the hillside. There we made the most of one last drink, our laughter carrying into the cold midnight sky.

Escaping the Monochrome Closet at Pride

Jane Aerith Magnet

Forty, trans woman, online entertainer and writer

In June 2010, I came out as trans for the second time. The first time I had gone back into the closet due to a complete lack of support from my family, and I was determined not to let that happen again. I was thirty years old and my grandmother – who'd done most of the actual raising of me – had died a few years prior. As such, I found myself caring far less what my remaining family thought. I was going to come out and they were not going to stop me.

Earlier in the year I'd arranged my first deed poll. It was a way to separate myself from my parents, with whom there had always been a distance. Included as a middle name was Jane, much to the bemusement of work's HR department, who grilled me on it numerous times to confirm they'd logged my details correctly. I get it: it's not common for someone to have Mr and Jane in their name at the same time. It was a stepping stone.

In the preceding months I'd started experimenting more with the way I dressed in public. Much more colour, more gender-neutral styles, often wearing skirts out clubbing with friends. None of it was particularly feminine, but it was a wild freedom of style that was certainly different enough to draw alternate cheers and confused looks. Just as with my family, I didn't much care what people thought. My confidence had really started to soar at that time, and I don't think I could have come out at all if that hadn't been the case. I was riding a self-confidence high, and it was propelling me through the early stages of transition.

However, going full-time as a trans woman and beginning the Herculean task of seeking assistance through the NHS with the medical side of transition, I found dealing with the general public on a day-to day basis to be rather gruelling. The 'I don't care what they think' attitude was ground down by a system that made it hard to ignore others' perceptions of myself, and where those perceptions could make the difference between my safety and being at risk.

It wasn't making me want to detransition; I wanted to transition but not to be noticed at all. The colour drained out of me as much as it did from my wardrobe. Gone were the neon long socks, the greens, purples, pinks of everyday wear. Gone was the blonde streak through my hair, the brightly coloured bag. Stopping people noticing me meant I didn't have to face their reactions to me.

All that remained was black leggings, muted grey tops and black cardigans. I'd stopped dressing like my cis friends – whose styles I admired and hoped to incorporate – and started dressing like my high-school drama teacher. I used to say, 'I don't wear make-up because I'm not out to impress anyone.' Over time I instead started spending around forty-five minutes on my face in the morning, shaving several times – just to be sure – and then plastering layer upon layer of foundation on to hide the horror of my own face.

Eventually I took down or covered every mirror in my house. I could shave by touch alone, and I had a tiny hand mirror for putting on make-up, not large enough for me to see more than a few inches of face at any given time. That way I could separate myself from what I saw.

Should anyone say anything about any possible facial hair shadow in the street, that was me done; I was heading to the nearest public toilet to carefully reapply my layers of make-up and hide myself again, before heading home to hide, cry and hate myself for things I had no real control over.

For years I didn't touch my face for fear of smudging or rubbing make-up off in some area. An itch was never met with scratching, just careful and precise pokes with my fingernail. It's such a simple thing that I just couldn't do for fear that someone would notice and say something.

My war on my own hair locked me further and further away from living my life. Sometimes I'd be so self-conscious as to have to spend my lunch breaks doing another shave and reapplying make-up. If I was invited anywhere last minute, I always had to decline. No after-parties, no impromptu nights out, no sudden day trips. I had to be sure my face wasn't showing, had to know where I could go in a hurry if I even began to suspect that it would start showing, and I had to know how to get home quickly if my fear couldn't be held in check any longer.

Because of the glacial pace at which UK gender services move, I was unable to start hormones until five years into my transition (I would genuinely love to know where trans-exclusionary reactionaries get the idea it's a fast or easy-to-breeze-through process). I'd had to learn to survive on my own in the wild, and this was mostly done by hiding from the world and myself as much as possible.

Every year in November the trans community join together to remember those who didn't make it: those victims of violence based on bias against trans people from around the world. If you're feeling strong emotionally, I strongly recommend everyone attend a Transgender Day of Remembrance (TDoR) event at least once. Depending on the event you attend, there may be one or all of the following: a list of names read – sometimes including the cause of death – lighting of candles, music, poetry and speeches.

In 2015 I headed to central London for one such event. I went alone, straight after a visit to the gender-identity clinic. Sitting in a large lecture theatre at one of the universities, surrounded by strangers, many wearing purple as a mark of respect, I listened and watched as the names of the fallen were read and a candle lit for each. The list never seemed to end: 217 people snuffed out for the perceived crime of being trans. Children murdered by parents, teens murdered by peers, lovers murdered by their partners. I don't think I've ever felt quite so emotionally wrung out. It's hard not to feel absolute blind anger at the injustice of the whole thing. While this was the first time I'd been so near to so many other trans people (several hundred), I was not at all comforted by it. It was on that night I heard a saying that has never left me: 'They say in Brazil that there are no old trans people, because they don't live that long.'

At this point in my transition, I needed some hope. I was hiding myself away from the world, trying not to be seen, and fixated on the worst of what can happen to the transgender community. I found that hope the following summer.

In July 2016 I went to my first Trans Pride event in Brighton. At that time Trans Pride had been running about three years and had grown significantly from its humble roots as a tiny event tucked away in a tiny green space and only lightly attended.

As was typical, I'd had anxiety even leaving the house and so arrived a little later than I'd originally intended. A cis friend – who'd offered to come with me for moral support – and I took the train down to the coast, along the way chatting about anything that wasn't the day so as not to get too anxious.

We hurried off of the train at the other end and jogged down the hill towards the beach. I knew we'd missed the start of the march (a crowd I wasn't capable of managing, I was certain) but was hoping we could join up somewhere on the main road along the seafront. What I saw surprised me: a much larger march than I'd expected for the event, taking up space. A privilege I'd been denying myself for some years now.

At last we came to Brunswick Gardens, the venue for the rest of the afternoon. The crowd filing into the park looked huge, and there were more to come as the rest of the march made its way in. Despite the numbers, there was plenty of space and no pushing – something that terrifies me about going to large demonstrations. It was in this crowd I finally started to take in those around me.

People of all ages and genders. There were people like me, my age and younger. There were more trans men than I'd ever encountered, even in online communities. There were non-binary folks, intersex people. There were goths, ravers, hippies, punks, trans people with physical disabilities, trans people of colour, sex workers. All in one physical place that wasn't an internet forum.

It was a far cry from the plasticky, corporate gloss of a lot of other pride events I've attended. Less noticeably white-dominated, more even representation across a whole spectrum of humanity. And heck, these people had passion and power about them that was contagious.

I'd not been one for speaking up for a few years at that point. Always wanting to be quiet, safe in my invisibility, but in that crowd I had a voice to chant with them, to shout with them and to speak up for what everyone there was voicing.

Eventually the crowd moved forward, and my friend and I made our way into the park itself. We looked around the stalls, listened to music and poetry from the main stage, and enjoyed the sun, which smiled down on us. As the day wore on however, the usual fears started to creep in. The sun was beating down and I was starting to worry about my make-up sliding off my face, so I headed to the toilet queue so I could quickly hide there and fix any possible issues.

About halfway to the Portaloo queue, standing just off a pathway, I was struck by a thought that absolutely knocked me for six. I burst into sudden tears, which surprised me. Not tears of sadness though – of relief and joy. For the first time in six years of being out and trans, here I was at a busy event, and I knew, I knew right to my very core, that not one single soul in that park cared whether or not I was showing a shadow through my make-up, or even if I had any on at all. In that moment I felt such a weight lifted from my shoulders. I felt so free to be me, without apology or needing to be ready to explain myself to anyone who might have a problem with my transness. No need to be on edge for fear that someone would attack me for being who I am while out in public. And as tears flowed down my face, I closed my eyes, smiled up at the sun, which smiled down on me, and hugged myself for a moment, knowing that things would be okay, even if only for that afternoon.

Since that day I've very much found my colours again. My hair has been neon shades of green and pink; it's been red, purple and yellow. My wardrobe is now filled with a spectrum of colours. That day in the park, surrounded by such an array of transness, helped with a lot of much-needed healing, which has continued to this day.

Loving My Deep Voice as Performance Rather Than Default

Laura Kate Dale

As a trans woman, the first time I really thought about my voice was when I started undergoing testosterone-based puberty in my teens. Growing up, my voice had always just sort of been a background aspect of my life, something I didn't really give much consideration. It was a baseline, it was familiar, it wasn't gendered in any way that really drew my attention, or that of anyone around me. It was the only voice I'd ever had, and it was mine.

That obviously changed when testosterone invited itself into my life. My voice dropped pretty hard, pretty fast, and to put it lightly, I was not a fan. My voice felt alien to me, and it was a big source of early dysphoria during puberty. When I would speak, it felt like picking a dialogue option in a video game, and hearing someone else's voice lines play. There was a level of disconnect between my voice and my sense of self.

When I think about the dysphoria I felt around my voice dropping, a lot of it centred around how that new voice applied to my internal sense of self. It wasn't my voice, it didn't feel like me, and as a result I did my best to push it away and pretend it didn't exist. I spent years working on gently raising my vocal pitch, making an effort to learn how to get my voice to naturally sit somewhere that felt more gender-affirming. Day to day, my speaking voice needed to be something that felt inherently me, like it wasn't a character whose voice I was making use of.

However, this story at its core isn't about my struggles with disliking the deeper end of my vocal range, it's about how, over the past few years, I have come to love that voice again, by getting some distance from it, and seeing it for the performance it is.

It was 2017, around seven or eight years after I first started coming out to my family and friends as trans. I'd spent enough of the previous decade working on changing my voice, and a fairly big percentage of people in my life who had not known me pre-puberty had no real scale for how much my voice had changed between it initially dropping and me making attempts to bring its pitch back up. I knew the changes were pretty major, thanks to old recordings of myself on my computer, but the changes had been gradual enough that a lot of people who heard my voice regularly hadn't really noticed them as they happened.

I had also been podcasting weekly for several years at this point, and my voice was apparently in the sort of space I wanted it to be, as a lot of people who listened to me on podcasts were unaware of my trans status until

I opted to bring it up on my own terms. I had found a voice I could comfortably relax into, and one I didn't feel dysphoric about.

At this point in my life, dropping my voice back down to its old teenage vocal range was a bit of a party trick I would sometimes make use of around close friends. It took some effort, thought and practice, but I could get my voice to drop down to an almost caricaturishly deep register, which certainly clashed a little with my outward presentation at the time. I would be wearing a dress and denim jacket, long hair swept across my face, and suddenly drop my voice so it sounded like that of a bad male extra from a British soap opera. I thought it was funny; the jarring change in my voice was to me pretty amusing, a sign of how far I had come.

The reactions I would get to showing off my old voice were always a little bit mixed from cisgender friends and family. Some found it impressive how much my voice had changed, just as I had hoped they might. Some found that it didn't seem to fit with my face, finding amusement in the juxtaposition between what they expected and what they were hearing. Some went as far as to tell me it made them feel uncomfortable. For those who found it uncomfortable, their reasons very much mirrored those I had when my voice first dropped: it didn't seem like it was my voice. It was unsettling hearing the wrong voice come out of my face. Hearing that others felt that way about me revisiting my old voice reminded me of a lot of baggage I had about that voice, and that stuck with me a bit.

The mixed nature of reactions to my vocal party trick discouraged me for a long time from playing around in the lower end of my vocal register, but it was another trans woman, my wife-to-be, Jane (author of the previous essay in this anthology), who finally helped me find some joy and pride in the voices I was able to produce.

I remember the morning in question really clearly. I had travelled to stay with Jane, who I wasn't yet living with, for a long weekend together. We had a rave we both wanted to attend in London, and decided I would come up to hers, we would go for the night out together and spend the following day just chilling in bed, catching up on sleep and bingeing TV together. A day with no set commitments, just reruns of cartoons we had both seen before, so if one of us needed to crash out for a bit more sleep we wouldn't miss anything too important. There were snacks on hand, a lot of cuddles to be shared, and a lot of silly chat.

Now, Jane had always been a fan of doing silly voices – it was kind of her thing. She used to perform stand-up comedy, and sometimes creates sketch-comedy videos online, and as a result she's always been a fountain of caricaturish voices. It's one of my favourite things about her. From the 'Drunken Sherry Lady', a shrill, high-pitched and slightly slurred feminine voice, to the voice of an invisible weather reporter, Jane's regular use of exaggerated voices never failed to bring a smile to my face. She pulled me into it too, encouraging me to try voices with her. We would frequently slip into the sherry lady voices while cooking dinner, or playing through video games together. We would slip in and out of voices sometimes without even meaning to. They were that big a part of our shared life.

At some point during this sleepy, cuddly morning, Jane and I got to talking about the silly voices we did and, more specifically, the voices we didn't do. Both of us had this massive part of our vocal range we didn't ever really play around with, for fear people who were not us would respond with confusion. We had this big chunk of sounds we were capable of producing but didn't make use of because of external perceptions. Both of us had this weird lingering fear around playing with deep or masculine voices, and we were both pretty sad about it.

So, on a sleepy morning, snuggled up together under blankets, we started workshopping a set of fictional male friends to voice, whose personalities and vocal ranges deliberately clashed in the same sort of ways people perceived our voices and presentations clashing. They were traditional British lads, with deep, gruff voices and a love for traditionally masculine-coded pursuits, but also a love for aspects of life not typically societally coded as masculine. Barry and Larry, in their low, rumbling voices, discussed how nice it can be to get a manicure done, or how much they've been enjoying reading housekeeping magazines, or going out dancing with their friends. They were a pair of men whose personalities were masculine-coded voices juxtaposed with a comfort in their masculinity that allowed them to love what they loved without fearing judgement.

These characters eventually morphed over the weeks

that followed and became a pair we now tend to refer to as the Brocial Justice Warriors, a pair of tough-as-nails British lads who care very much about improving the state of the world.

Here's the thing about playing around with masculine voices: I never hated the voice testosterone gave me, I just hated that it was my everyday voice. It was an alien voice, and I didn't want it to be the voice I used when seeing friends, or while at work, or when on the phone. I didn't want it to be the voice that people used to understand who I was, but the voice itself wasn't inherently a bad one.

After that the floodgates opened and we started to realise we had a bunch of other silly voices now open to us that we had previously been missing out on. We began to play around with voices for fake video-game-industry executives, game-show hosts, nasty old rich men with too much money and power, and a whole bunch more. We gave ourselves permission to play around with what our voices could do, free of any risk of judgement or fear that we would be seen as less inherently female for engaging with our old voices. It was incredibly liberating.

Ultimately, what made this story one of gender euphoria for me was the impact it had on the rest of my relationship to my voice.

For the longest time, when I was first coming out as trans, I felt a real pressure for my voice to always be as high-pitched as I could comfortably and naturally get it to go. I felt that if I wasn't doing everything possible to erase the voice I once had, I wasn't being trans the right way.

That's nonsense, and it took revisiting the rest of my vocal range to see that.

My voice is what it is. I went through a testosterone puberty and oestrogen hormone replacement therapy won't undo that. Rather than worrying that my voice still isn't high enough, I can look at how far it has come, and use that as a reassuring barometer that my voice today is okay. Not pretending that part of my vocal range doesn't exist has allowed me to take much greater ownership over my new day-to-day speaking voice. My speaking voice is my real voice, and my old voice is now what it always felt like – a performance, a character, something that isn't who I am.

Separating out my old voice, and assigning it to a fictional silly character I can perform, really helped me to feel secure and joyous in the knowledge that my being female isn't undermined by the fact I can make myself sound like a hired goon in a heist movie.

It took having another trans woman explore voices with me to open me up to the idea that my deeper vocal range could be something I might one day love, from a safe and respectable distance. As a character voice, I love that part of my range. It's a tool in an arsenal of very silly voices Jane and I use day to day, and just by virtue of it being a character's voice rather than mine, I can see it for what it is: a voice to be loved rather than scorned.

The Euphoria That Lies in Revolt: Loving Myself While Living in Brazil

Júlia F. Cândida

Twenty-two, trans woman making movies in Goiás, Brazil

On 10 October 2018 I wrote a comment on a transgender subreddit post talking about the rise in popularity of then-presidential candidate Jair Bolsonaro – who I would call a fascist – and what that would mean for the trans people living in Brazil. I will show you the comment now, with some of the misspellings corrected and the translation of the Brazilian term used in it updated.

Hello, I'm from Brazil, and I wanted to share my story somewhere.

I am a bisexual and transgender girl, not as openly as I would want to be, but I do go out at night with my friends wearing clothes that I actually enjoy wearing and stuff ... Basically, I've spent nineteen years of my life living on a pretty tight leash, and when I finally moved away (for college, that is), my experiments with sexuality and gender started, and I feel like my anxieties and depression have drastically decreased since then.

But now with this political climate change, I fear that someone will try to do something bad to me or my friends (that are mostly gay, Black and/or 'leftists', as they would say). This is not a new feeling for me, even though I have been doing this gender experimentation for only a little less than a year. However, with a candidate that literally said recently that he will '*fuzilar a petralhada*' ('gun down his political adversaries' – or basically, everyone that disagrees with him or his methods) … I am more worried about my safety than ever before. I fear that someone might shoot me, I fear that they might harm my friends, and worst of all, I fear that I am going to end up hurting myself if this oppression gets stronger.

I am only partially out of my gender closet, and I do not want to go back. (…) I just wanted to share this somewhere. Thank you for your time. Ele Não.

At the time I was not as open about my gender identity as I would be roughly a year later, but I knew I was already in his crosshairs when Bolsonaro made that comment. I see people describing him as 'the Latin-American version of Donald Trump', and even though there are some disagreements on which of them is actually the worst one, for the purposes of this essay it fits as a good descriptor for him. Historically speaking, Brazil is infamous for mistreating its transgender community. Even though we have seen some progress, such as the possibility of having gender-reassignment surgery on the public health system and the ruling that allowed us to change our legal name even without professional evaluation or surgery, Brazil has the highest transgender murder rate on the planet, according to TGEU (Transgender Europe), an NGO. In addition, events such as 1987's Operação Tarântula, during which over 300 trans women were arrested, and the cruel murder of Dandara dos Santos in 2017, show how much living in Brazil can still be a challenge.

Living in this context, Jair Bolsonaro's election felt like a punch to the face, particularly when paired with his insistence on using fearmongering tactics to demonise LGBTQIA+ people, such as the (unfortunately common) accusation that we aim to sexualise and also 'brainwash' younglings to make them follow left-wing beliefs. In this demonisation, transgender people are made easy targets for allegedly spreading 'gender ideology' and turning innocent people trans themselves. Not only that, but his open approval of the Brazilian military-dictatorship period – in which thousands were tortured, murdered and had their bodies disposed of in secrecy – makes it clear that our democracy has been hanging by a thread ever since the results of the election came in.

So I find myself in a weird position regarding the year 2018, given it was the year that everything seemed to get worse, but it was also the year that I finally found out I am a transgender woman. Therefore, I went through a great deal of happiness which was interspersed with a similarly great deal of uncertainty and fear for my life during those twelve months.

Even though it was a chaotic year in the grand scheme of things, I feel that I should not let the good memories wash away in the torrential rain, while obviously not ignoring said rain. To talk about my euphoria I need to make the other side of the coin clear.

So, it was 2018 and I was just turning twenty years old. While I had spent many years trying to ignore feelings I had around gender, this was the year I decided to finally experiment in earnest, and work out how I felt about my gender, rather than trying to purposely ignore those thoughts and feelings I had spent years struggling with. At that time, I was living alone, far away from my parents, starting my second year in film school, which had broadened my horizons on the ways people could express themselves politically and in terms of their own sexuality or gender. Being around people that were open-minded about these topics was essential for me to figure out who I was. I moved to my new home somewhat aware that I wasn't only able to be attracted to women, and managed to confirm that in the very first year. However, maybe due in part to a lack of contact with other transgender people, I initially felt a lot less able to experiment with those aspects of myself.

When my birthday came, I remember that I wanted to take that doubt out of my head, and confirm whether I was trans or not. In retrospect, maybe a cisgender person wouldn't spend as much of their life as I did considering whether they would feel less miserable if they were assigned the opposite gender from the one they were born with. That probably should have been a pretty clear clue, in retrospect.

So, while it might not seem like a huge step to some, on my birthday I shaved my beard, which I had been growing since 2015. I cannot deny how good that small feat made me feel at the time, although keeping my face clean of hair started to become an annoying chore. Necessary, but annoying nonetheless.

At that time, there were only a few people in my life aware of my dissatisfaction in being socially read as a man, and I cannot stress enough how much they helped me, especially the few high-school friends that I still keep in touch with.

A few days after my birthday, a girl who was starting her first year in film school moved in next door to me, and we quickly became friends. So much so that it did not take long for me to talk to her about my wish to see how I would feel about wearing a dress and make-up. I knew that wouldn't necessarily 'turn me into a woman', but I wanted to see how I would look. I wanted to see a different version of myself.

Aware of that, on 12 March she asked me if I would like to help her test her makeover skills. Since that was a win-win scenario, I agreed. I remember that when she was done, I looked at the mirror and realised I looked a bit like another friend of mine, and then I noticed that I actually felt very attractive, which was a first for me.

Maybe that was when I finally noticed how much I used to avoid acknowledging that I hardly ever felt good about myself. The idea that I could be satisfied with my image always seemed impossible, because I never considered that I could reach that point, as if the dissatisfaction would never go away. I always enjoyed creating little escapisms for myself, playing only female characters in video games and at one point only writing stories with female main characters (the name Júlia comes from one of them), always wanting to be someone else rather than me. I am aware that this awakening was probably too centred on the gender binary at the time, but it was when I started to actually look deep inside and ask myself important questions, such as: When I get older, do I really want to look like my grandfather or my grandmother? For some reason this question really pushed me over the edge.

So, back to that night trying out make-up, I was feeling hot! What the fuck? Apparently, I *am* allowed to feel this way. What a concept. My friend saw that I was enjoying myself, so she lent me a dress, which also looked good on me. She also called another friend of ours to film an improvised interview with me, given we were film students, after all. Unfortunately, I think we lost the footage when her laptop developed a problem and she had to clean her hard drive. I need to ask her, but I am too afraid to know the truth. I really hope a record of that euphoric night still exists somewhere, kept safe.

After that day I received a self-esteem boost that lasted quite a while. While I was on this high, I went on a trip with my dad to São Paulo, where I bought my first dress, using the excuse that it was for a friend. In addition to that, I got the chance to watch the 2017 film *Una Mujer Fantastica* (*A Fantastic Woman*), which was such a great experience that I still remember how it all felt. The movie tells the story of a transgender woman dealing with the tragic loss of her partner while having to deal with his transphobic family, who want to prevent her being at his funeral. I really don't think I've ever felt so immersed in a film before, and having watched it just a few days after figuring out I was trans definitely made the experience in itself extremely touching and memorable.

Given our poor representation in the media in general, seeing an actual transgender actress (Daniela Vega) playing the main character, in a story that doesn't look down on her or judge her just on account of her gender identity, while not pulling back on depicting the massive hurdles she goes through caused by transphobia, was really powerful to me.

Watching that film definitely made me feel a bit more at ease with the personal revelations I was coming to regarding my gender. Seeing a character facing the cruelty of a society that truly does not want us around, and watching her have an ending that is – all things considered – a happy ending, was something I didn't know I needed. My immersion in the story was so strong that when the credits started rolling, I had to take a minute to come back to myself. It might feel a little weird to consider my experience watching this movie as a moment of gender euphoria, but it reminded me how powerful good representation can be to a person that doesn't normally fit in.

Three months later I was still taking my time to process what my transition would mean for me and for all the other aspects of my life. I was very cautious about mentioning it to other people, while thinking about when I would work up the courage to wear the dress I bought in São Paulo and start to refer to myself as Júlia. Then, the 2018 FICA (the Brazilian International Environmental Film and Video Festival) started, and I knew my time had come.

My town, which usually tends to be very slow and quiet, gets crowded with tourists when the festival happens, full of people coming from in and out of the country. There were so many people that the idea of going to a few parties publicly as a woman came up very quickly. I think I used the excuse of this being a 'special occasion' for me to have the guts to do it, but I was probably just waiting for *any* kind of occasion to wear that cool dress in public.

Let me talk a bit about that dress, because it is almost perfect. It is white with orange flowers, and the skirt stops at the middle of my thighs. Sadly it does not fit my shoulders very well, or at least that's what I felt when I wore it on the day. That is one of the major flaws with the 'I'm buying this for a friend' excuse: having to guess my size, and with no chance of going to a changing room because I really did not want to out myself at the time.

So yeah, I panicked about how it fit on my shoulders, but after trying an opened-up red flannel shirt on top of the dress, it worked fine. It would cover my shoulders and protect me from the cold, which was a plus. Every time I looked at the mirror, the choice of clothing seemed more and more appealing and practical. I felt at peace.

That night, when I went out for the first time as Júlia, I learned so much about myself. Before even setting foot out of the house, I created many expectations about the types of reactions I was going to get. The good ones and the bad ones. Most of the people that knew me already were very friendly to me, and given that I had been a part of their lives for just a little more than a year, they got used to my new name and pronouns very quickly.

That night was also the first time I was able to tell exactly who *really* did not want me around them. I stayed close to my friends all the time because everything was so new and surprisingly unexpected to me. People staring at me was something that I had to get used to, and is the reason why I carry a pocketknife in my purse nowadays. I really cherish the good reactions I got that day, though.

Earlier that year, before I was out as a trans woman, someone introduced me to a girl who straight up told me: 'Holy crap, you are exactly my type. If I weren't a lesbian, we would totally hook up,' which left me delighted. I met her that day at the film festival, and the first thing she told me? 'Fuck, yeah, I knew it. You look really hot.'

As I mentioned before, the concept that I could be attractive to others and to myself never made too much sense to me before I realised I was trans. That night I saw people showing they were attracted to me, which felt good. However, when it came from a woman attracted to other women, I felt amazing. I am not only a woman, but a hot one, apparently. Double validation! My power grew immensely.

To be completely honest, this part is very difficult to write, because that night at the film festival, for all its wonderful memories, also ended in a very scary and upsetting way. As wonderful as that night was, I need to talk about how it ended, because I feel that if I don't address it here, it'll be like it never happened. To talk about my experiences of euphoria properly, I need to contrast the good with the bad.

So, as the day at the film festival continued, we went to a party that was happening near the movie theatre. The place was crowded and the DJ was playing 'music for gay people' (his words, not mine). We were having a good time, until suddenly a police car stopped outside the bar. Three cops got out and started to approach the crowd. One of them rudely bumped me with his shoulder while he was walking, like... well, like a cop. They went into the crowd, the music stopped, and all of a sudden they started yelling. After a few seconds, they reappeared from the crowd, taking a man with them.

After they left, someone told me what happened: the man dropped a gun on the dance floor and didn't even bother to hide that it was his. I imagine that maybe this kind of thing happens a lot in big cities, but the crime rate in our town is stupidly low. What reason did he have to be messing around with a gun in the middle of a dance floor? I have no reason to believe that he wanted to use it on me personally, but I don't have reason to believe I was perfectly safe either.

I was still afraid that something bad would happen to me that day. What made matters worse is that half an hour later three cop cars pulled up at the front of the bar. It turned out that after they took that man away, they let him go, still armed, and he immediately went back to the same place!

The owner of the bar called the police (again) and this time, instead of taking him away, they told the DJ to stop the music because 'the party is over'. No, of course they did not take the gunman away for a second time. They just left him there – possibly still armed – and left.

I said that this night paved the way for my understanding of how people were going to treat me, and that rings true here: the police do not care about us. Not one bit. It does not matter if they call themselves 'diverse'. If that place had a majority of white heterosexual cisgender people, I would bet that they would put him in jail the first time they were called to the club.

Remembering this makes me scared, and it makes me angry. It feels hard to talk about this moment, but I need to highlight it because it will probably happen again, and being silent about it will only make things worse.

We went to another place after all of that, but my friends did not want to stay for long. They were probably burned out by the whole situation, which I can understand. I wanted to stay longer to wash the memory away and have some fun so that wasn't my lingering memory of the night, but I did not feel safe staying alone there, so we left together.

Shortly after that night, our July break started. I went back to my home town to stay with my mom until the end of the month. She did not know about me being trans, so while I stayed there, I was constantly trying to drop hints about it without actually telling her. It obviously did not work, and it was only a year later that I got the courage to break the news.

One thing I managed to do while back at home was go to a thrift store and buy myself another dress that I found cute: a simple plain black dress. This one is more comfortable for me to wear, and I used a variant of the 'buying for a friend' excuse: the 'buying for an independent movie which I am working on as an art director's assistant'. I mean, I was doing just that, but the dress was obviously for me. My mother either believed it or did not want to ask questions that could lead to certain answers. My dad understood immediately what I was doing when buying that dress, but he had picked up on the fact I was trans a lot more easily than Mom, so he didn't question it.

When the break was over, I went back to the town that knew me by my name. My neighbour wanted to visit a mutual friend of ours with me, and when I was changing clothes to go there, I simply wore the black dress and went with her to his house. I still felt giddy because that dress fit wonderfully on my pre-HRT body, but it also felt normal, in a good way. Not dreading the way I looked was slowly starting to be common.

Things stayed normal until around October, when it became clear that Bolsonaro had the better chances to be the next president of Brazil. We had nationwide protests against him, where the chant 'Ele Não' ('Not Him') started to appear. His fanatical followers became even more unbearable, to the point that many friendships were lost and many family reunions became more unfriendly than they usually were.

Listening to people calling for 'gay genocide' became common, and people cheered their beloved fascist's name while they stabbed a transgender woman to death in São Paulo, while they assaulted a public worker in Recife, a young woman in Porto Alegre, a student in Curitiba. Every day we would hear about someone suffering at the hands of his supporters. After the election, you could feel the tension around us.

My immediate sadness turned to grief, which eventually turned into anger. I do not say that in a bad way, because being complacent in the face of all the injustice and constant threats against democracy made by the Bolsonaro family (three of his five children also hold positions of power within his government) is what made this country get in the mess we are in right now.

Anger not as in hate, but as a tool of self-defence.

The Brazil that was already failing us, even during so-called 'leftist governments', had decided that we had it too good for too long, apparently. With the country heading in a dark and worrying direction, I decided that I did not want to wait any longer for people to know me only as Júlia. We only live once, and since we are all in danger, I do not intend to take any regrets to my grave. I'm not going to live in fear and let that stop me living my life.

My experience talking to other transgender people as a trans woman myself confirmed that we are all fucking angry, and if we are not, we absolutely *should* be. We *have* to be angry.

The experience of looking back at 2018 so I could write this essay was interesting for me. Remembering the first few months after I finally listened to that interior voice telling me that I would be happier as a girl reminded me of how much I grew, and how much meeting other transgender people and living my own truths made me feel good.

Frankly, thinking back on 2018 was also stressful, a bit triggering, and made me want to get out and live new stories to tell. I write this, however, in 2020, a year that is not well suited to going out and making new memories.

All I can say is that 2018 Júlia feels like a different person from me today in many ways. Everything was new to me: going to thrift shops looking for good clothes and even hearing the name 'Júlia' used to send shivers down my spine. These things still bring me joy, but they are not new any more. I constantly feel like a woman, even though I do not pass that much. It seems like the 2018 me was just a kid, trying to understand what it meant to be a woman and how the world works for us.

Right now it feels like I've hit the teenage years, which means I am still trying to grasp those concepts, but my knowledge has increased since then, and I can be more adventurous in discovering who I am. While I lost some friends in 2018, I reconnected with others and bonded with some that I didn't have much contact with before, to the point that nowadays my friendship group is filled with supportive, trustworthy and wonderful people.

I feel more confident about myself: as an independent woman, as an artist, as someone who can be different in many ways and still have worth. My perception of myself is still changing in some ways that I cannot describe exactly yet, and that makes me very excited about what's to come. Somehow I feel hope. Maybe because, despite everything, I'm still going to be myself, and there's no one else I would rather be right now.

Thank you for your time, and of course: Ele Não.

The Gender of Language: Finding a Pronoun for My Identity

Teddy Sweet

Thirty, non-binary immigrant writer
enjoying village life in the UK

Growing up in Hungary, the concept of gender was not something that ever truly crossed my mind. The language is perfectly gender-neutral, which means that it was never an issue to correct assumptions in conversation or run the risk of getting a pronoun wrong. Really, the only time gender came up in life was when my father would sigh, 'Oh, my son. My daughter. My whatever,' to express light-hearted disappointment. I don't think he ever realised how spot on he was, because he did end up with three children: a son, a daughter and a 'whatever'.

To this day I'm not sure my dad truly knows that he has a spectrum of children: an eldest daughter, a non-binary middle child and a youngest son. It might be because we speak in Hungarian, but, by the same virtue, I have never expressly told him either. We're both happier not worrying about trying to find the right words to explain the concept of being non-binary. To us it makes no difference: we're still the same people, and, in Hungarian, it wouldn't change anything because there are no gendered pronouns. That's not to say I haven't dropped hints but, historically, my attempts to drop hints about things have not always been successful.

For example, I've been married for almost seven years now. Right from the start my husband and I were always pointing out good-looking people to each other, talking about celebrity crushes growing up, and I was quite open about appreciating all genders. Not once did I think that I was being discreet. However, it was only after six years and nine months of marriage that we were sitting on the sofa and my husband looked at me with mild confusion when I talked about the fluidity of sexuality and he asked, 'Teddy, are you bi?' Needless to say, we had a rather enlightening conversation and I had to rethink the quality of my hinting.

The first time I truly had to consider gender was when my family emigrated to the UK. Obviously I knew that there were girls and boys, but my childhood didn't revolve around being encouraged to behave one way or another. I could be foraging for snails and biking one day then going to folk-dancing classes the next. Moving to a new country was a bit eye-opening. I didn't speak much of the language, and the concept of gender pronouns was one that took a long while to get used to. It felt absolutely unnecessary and an additional challenge to overcome when trying to settle into a new life with a new language.

However, I'm pleased to say that I managed it, even if it still sometimes catches me out and I have to think really hard about who I'm talking about and which pronouns to use. It's not something that comes naturally to me.

One boon of it, though, is that I've found it relatively easy to change pronouns when friends have come out to me. I certainly slip up from time to time but, on the whole, it hasn't given me too much of a problem to adjust. This is likely because I am so used to having to think about which pronoun to use for someone, it's a conscious choice rather than reflexive habit, so I'm less likely to accidentally default to the wrong pronouns.

As an aside, I will say that one of the most rewarding moments of a friendship was when a close and trusted friend asked that I use he/him pronouns in relation to him. The happiness and contentment that shone through him the first time he was referred to by masculine pronouns was quite humbling. It is such a simple act to affirm someone's gender but it brings so much positivity for all.

In contrast, and perhaps because of my first language being gender-neutral, I never put too much stock into my own pronouns; they never brought me comfort or joy to use. I was ambivalent, at best, towards them, accepting that it was a necessity to be able to communicate in a grammatically correct way. Being referred to by one gender over another was something that I went along with, even if it never felt quite right. I was definitely fortunate to not have a strong, visceral reaction to this binary pigeonholing; instead, I learned to step over it and ignore the implications. A pronoun didn't define me; it simply made the lives of those around me easier.

That was until I discovered that they/them was becoming an acceptable third-person singular pronoun in English. Discovering it was a bit of a fluke. I had been cautiously dabbling in internet communities and was ever so hesitant to reveal anything personal. I didn't share anything: not my name, not my age, and not even my gender. This led to those who I now consider my friends referring to me as they/them, which was quite the revelation. I found that I liked it. Beyond simple liking, actually, to the point that I encouraged it because it resonated with me. Initially I thought it was because it harked back to Hungarian and the lack of gender specification in my native tongue. However, the more I thought about it, the more I realised it was definitely something on top of that. They/them felt right in a way no other pronoun in English had before.

The next natural step was to actively introduce myself with they/them pronouns. Initially, it was scary to even think about, so I started small: presenting myself to new, small communities as they/them. Nobody batted an eyelid, and the friends I made through writing events and challenges were all very accepting when I told them that I feel more comfortable not just with they/them pronouns but being recognised as a non-binary person. The biggest reaction I had from a friend was being given a non-binary flag pin in recognition of my gender. That pin still sits in my desk, a reminder for the not-so-great days that I have friends out in the world who knew me from before I came out, and after, and – aside from which pronouns they use for me – nothing has changed. Our friendships are the same as they have always been, and me opening up to them has only brought us closer, because I can be myself without having to hide or worry any more. By telling them I was non-binary, I no longer felt like a fraud for using they/them without acknowledging why I preferred such pronouns.

Despite such an overwhelmingly positive reaction, there is a huge duality still present in my life. Namely, the dissonance between language and acceptance within my two cultures. I love Hungarian; I think it is an eloquent and wonderful language – definitely one of the most creative for swearing, from what I hear. Whenever I go back to Hungary, I stop having to worry about pronouns and gender. It is so freeing because I don't have to hide my gender among certain groups, and there are no linguistic pressures or misconceptions to either live up to or make an awkward denial of. 'Back home' I can be who I want to be without having to explain myself or correct anyone.

It is also heartbreaking. Over the last couple of years Hungary has been making quite large leaps in the wrong direction. As of May 2020, it has become impossible to legally change one's gender. There is no recognition for transgender people; the binary gender assigned at birth is the only one that is recognised by the state. This makes self-expression nigh on impossible, and very risky. Discrimination is rife, as is intolerance. To declare one's self as trans is to willingly open oneself up to attacks. It is inspiring to find that people still speak up, demanding that they be recognised for who they are, not what they were assigned, because their identity will not be erased by short-sighted bureaucracy.

The only saving grace of Hungary is the language. If there is a need to specify a gender, it has to be explicitly stated with 'that man' or 'that woman'. Of course there is an exception to the rule when speaking about roles and jobs, though this is a little outdated and has been slowly erased from the language. Given the current climate in the country surrounding trans rights, I suspect this is more to do with ease of speaking than with the feminist wave pushing to remove 'woman-specific' tags from the vernacular.

A general rule of thumb was that if a doctor is a man, he would be referred to as 'doctor' while if the doctor is a woman, she would be called 'doctor-woman'. The same thing would apply to actor/actress, policeman/policewoman and a handful of other roles. Interestingly, not all jobs have such a gender distinction: a builder is still a builder, not a builder-woman, while there is also no such thing as a psychologist-woman. The evolution of the language to gradually lose the '-woman' suffix is one that I personally welcome. It is nice to be referred to as a writer regardless of gender rather than having to explicitly declare my identity by differentiating between writer and writer-woman.

While I have not yet been in a situation in Hungary

where I've had to talk about being non-binary, it is something I both dread and am intrigued by. The very reason it is so easy to avoid gender-oriented conflict is also the downfall of having such a conversation. In the UK, I can explain my identity in simple terms. In Hungarian, I do not have the vocabulary for it. There is a wide, simplistic and very binary understanding of being transgender, in that it means to transition and live as the opposite gender from the one assigned at birth. Yet to explain that I am neither would, ironically, be facilitated by male and female pronouns to illustrate my point with sufficient impact. Though, given how English is only now coming to more widely accept they/them as a third person singular pronoun, it makes me wonder whether I would have had a harder time conveying the concept of being non-binary if I didn't have they/them so readily available to me.

The only time I came even close to trying to explain being non-binary in Hungarian was to my sister. We very quickly had to switch to English, not even realising at the time that we had changed languages.

Usually, if we're in a public setting, we speak Hungarian, confident that very few, if any, people will understand us. This means that our conversations are much more free and honest, not having to worry about those around us eavesdropping on a private moment. Sometimes, if a word doesn't come naturally to us in Hungarian, we substitute the English for it. This has led to a rather patchwork way of talking at times but, even with our fluency in both languages and ability to interchange the words as needed, it became obvious that English was more suited to express and explain everything.

By contrast, in the UK, and online, where I write in English, I've found that while the vast majority of people will refer to me as they/them if they're not certain which pronouns I prefer, there are some who decide what my gender is based on the presence they perceive I project. So both she/her and he/him have been used in relation to me. Though, I have to admit that my absolute favourites have been 'm'theydy' and 'gentlethem' from a couple of cheeky supporters. Even if they didn't realise just how right they were, their general joking ease with non-binary names was one that had me thoroughly entertained and pleased. The creativity and positivity of people never ceases to amaze me.

In English there is no omission of gender from everyday speech. Each time a gendered pronoun has been used to refer to me, I've had a choice to make. Either allow it to go ignored, hoping that over time my preference for gender-neutral would be noticed. Or I could engage and politely request that they/them is used when talking about me. Both have their advantages and their pitfalls. To ignore it is easier in the short term – I am ambivalent about gender, have no preference, and the non-binary label feels the most comfortable. It is how I identify myself, though some have suggested agender might be more fitting. To me it doesn't matter. I'm neither male nor female; some days I might be more one or the other but usually I'm happiest somewhere in between. This is probably why I do not have a strong reaction to being misgendered and what makes ignoring it easier for me. Truthfully, I get a bit of a kick out of it, seeing how people perceive me and my writing and the assumptions they draw.

While it is more difficult to approach someone, usually a stranger, with a gentle, 'Excuse me but they/them are my pronouns,' it can be another moment of quiet celebration of gender. Having the security and courage to turn around and freely discuss my identity with the expectation of being listened to and accepted is a huge privilege. Especially when I contrast my situation with what's happening in Hungary.

Even if such an interaction runs the risk of a negative response, I always live in hope that I'm approaching a fellow human being who, if treated with kindness even in the face of vitriol, might remember the exchange later in life. It is this hope that makes it worth putting myself out there, even if, in the immediate event, my request to be accepted on my terms is met with hostility; there's no telling what impact a polite and respectful interaction might have in the future.

Thankfully, I've found myself in communities and groups that are very accepting and, on the whole, people in general are also very appreciative of gender identity, so will try their utmost to remember how to address me. That's not to say there aren't slip-ups, but they're not malicious or deliberate, so it's easy to forgive. And when they correct themselves, with or without prompting, their affirmation of my identity is a quiet swell of happiness every single time.

I've had twenty-plus years to get used to gendered pronouns. It's only been in the last few years though that I've found a pronoun that feels right to me. There was no light-bulb moment where I switched. For me, it's been a quiet, slow trickle of settling and finding comfort in who I am. Which is where I am now. I know I have been very fortunate to get to a point where not only am I surrounded by people who accept me as I am, but that I also am at ease with myself. It has made quite the difference, though; I'm definitely happier and able to put my all into my writing, my volunteering and my family. It certainly feels like I'm going to get to live my happily ever after on my own terms.

This dichotomy of being from a country whose language gives absolute gender-neutrality yet seems intent on destroying all trans rights, while living in a country that is much more proactive about trans rights yet is only just starting to explore the idea of gender-neutral single-person pronouns, is not lost on me. It certainly feels like Hungary has a language that is ahead of its time, while the country is working its hardest to culturally regress on any advancements that have been made over the years. Meanwhile, the UK is slowly but surely trying to shed a completely binary speech pattern to allow language to catch up with current attitudes, and hopefully will continue to move in the correct direction, bringing more people the affirmation and euphoria they deserve.

Mentally Rewriting Life Before Surgery

Laura Kate Dale

Ever since I started undergoing testosterone-based puberty in my mid-teens, I disliked having a penis. It's not like it's an inherently bad part of the body, and having one certainly didn't make me any less valid as a trans woman, but it really just wasn't for me. It felt like something slapped onto me late in the design process to fill space, a placeholder, a random addition that wasn't really meant to be there. It wasn't something I had control over, and it wasn't something I ever felt any real positive feelings for. It just kind of existed. I ignored it as best I could until I learned there were options for it and I to part ways.

Undergoing vaginoplasty, an operation where the penis is surgically operated on to create a vagina in its place, is by no means a necessary end goal for all trans women. It's a very painful surgery, it takes either large amounts of money or jumping through medical gatekeeping hoops to access, and recovery after surgery is a months-long process. Beyond that, there are a lot of trans women who just don't feel any great dislike of their penis. I know some who love theirs, and they're just as valid as those of us who feel negatively. It wasn't for any societal expectation about what a woman should be that I opted to seek my vaginoplasty; it was just one of the steps on my personal journey I needed to feel more at peace with the body I had.

For me, having lower surgery was an important light at the end of the tunnel for my transition. It was a tangible end goal, the final time I was going to need the help of a doctor to get my body in line with what I wanted it to be. The final hurdle I would eventually have to climb, navigating the UK medical system as a trans woman.

The road to me getting my vagina installed was certainly a bit of a bumpy one. Simply getting referred to the gender identity clinic in London took years, there were a bunch of setbacks that kept delaying my treatment, and due to some issues with paperwork, I more than once found myself having to start waiting periods for certain milestone appointments over from scratch. While I took as many of those setbacks in my stride as I could, the one that eventually got to me was when I had to restart my two-year wait for lower surgery because an appointment letter arrived after the appointment it was for. Having not responded or cancelled because I had not received the letter was deemed me forfeiting my place in line.

I ended up undergoing lower surgery privately, an option that was only available to me thanks to the privilege I had as a trans woman who already had a decent-sized following as a writer. In the space of around ten days I raised enough money to pay for some private medical referrals, talk to a surgeon, and get myself booked in for my vaginoplasty. I had no trouble getting the needed referrals; I'd been out as Laura full time for several years at this point with a solid paper trail documenting my transition, and before I knew it this huge mythical end goal to the medical side of my transition was within arm's reach. It was a tangible thing. It was really going to happen.

Obviously, when I first found out I was finally going to be able to have lower surgery, I was ecstatic. It was pretty overwhelming emotionally. As a former avid swimmer who had refrained from swimming for fun for around a decade, the thought of being able to go swimming again brought me to tears more than once. I realised I was going to be able to throw out items of clothing I owned that were purely designed to flatten my crotch. I was going to be able to wear leggings without worrying about the shape of my crotch. I wasn't going to have to think, day to day, about how to make this part of my body stay as out of the way and unobtrusive as possible. I felt relief, joy and freedom, which I couldn't quite do justice with words.

Now, when it comes to my feelings about surgery as it drew closer, I'm not afraid to admit there were some moments where things were not all sunshine and rainbows. As much as I knew vaginoplasty was the right option for me, I'd had enough people in my life asking me if I was sure I wouldn't regret it, and enough doctors and surgeons warning me about horrible but incredibly rare complications, that I had some concerns leading up to surgery. What if I came out the other side and it wasn't everything I had dreamed? What if something went wrong in surgery that couldn't be repaired? What if it somehow didn't work? What if I actively hated the result?

I think all of these are healthy things to think about before undergoing major surgery. The fact that I was thinking about them pretty constantly before I went under, but I still went through with it, should tell you something about how strongly I knew it was the right thing for me personally. No matter how loud my worries and worst-case scenarios got, none of them were a bigger deal to me than the fact I knew that I wanted this.

When I first woke up after surgery, still groggy and delirious from the combination of different drugs pumped into my system, I was a real mix of ecstatic and concerned. I'd had an epidural to deal with some of the surgical pain, and I woke up a little bit worried that something had gone wrong because I couldn't feel my legs. But, apart from that needless worry, I was initially over the moon to look down at myself and see a flat section of bandages where previously my nemesis had been in residence.

I took a selfie of my face, completely undeterred by the fact I desperately needed a shave, a smile brimming from ear to ear, declaring to the world, 'I have a vagina!' The joy was pure; I knew in my heart I had done the right thing.

As amazing as that moment of joy coming out of surgery was, however, it's not actually the moment of gender euphoria I've been building to. As I said earlier, a vaginoplasty is a difficult surgery to recover from, and that moment of joy was brief. It was followed by a lot of difficult moments before things really settled back into a more reliable joy.

One thing that nobody really prepares you for, as a trans person who chooses to undergo lower surgery, are the emotional challenges that come in the immediate aftermath of surgery. You're in pain, you're exhausted, your crotch is a swollen, bloody mess, if you move you might tear something, and any romanticised daydreams about gently getting to know a new part of your body are going to need to wait a fair few months. Your body has a lot of healing to do, and at least for me, I was a little afraid to get too attached until things were all healed. I knew the road to recovery could take up to six months, but I didn't want my first real associations with my genitals to be their post-surgical state. I wanted to wait to get to know them until they were a bit more stable.

Additionally I had a lot of dreams, worrying that somehow my penis was going to return. Some surgeon was going to reverse it, or it would grow back, or a penis would simply fall out of me. These dreams persisted for a while, probably as a result of my brain trying to process some pretty major changes it had undergone, but I always woke up alarmed when it happened.

During those months of recovery I didn't always love my new vagina. It was there, it was a part of my life, but I didn't really engage with it too much. That went on for a while, while things healed up, but somewhere along the line, things began to change. The more my body healed, the more of an active interest I took in it. The more I acknowledged that my new body existed, the more comfortable I became with its role in my life.

With this all said, the moment that I truly felt gender euphoria after surgery was a really small and simple moment. Nothing flashy. The moment I remember most isn't the first time I went swimming post-surgery, or the day I woke up knowing it was done. It was the first time I realised I'd forgotten the part of my life before my vaginoplasty completely.

Now, let me be clear: I'm not saying I have a twenty-year gap in my memory, or that I am unaware of reality. I know, on paper, for the first couple of decades of my life, I had a penis. What I am saying is that, for as much as my penis seemed like a huge problem that needed overcoming while I had it, once it was gone I fell into a new sense of self that rippled back through my memories. Having a vagina felt so inherently right, so unambiguously how things were meant to be, that everything just clicked into place. It felt like the right genitals had always been there, just waiting to come to the surface.

It's a weird experience to try and describe. Before undergoing surgery I took a photograph of my penis, just to exist as a memory of what had previously been. Looking back on that photograph months later, it seemed almost comical. There was no way that had once upon a time been a part of my body. The thought of that being how I was born, and how I lived for twenty years, was laughable. It didn't make sense. That feeling of disconnect from my old genitals, the fact that my vagina simply felt like it had always been there, was a hugely validating experience. It made so much of my transition up to that point fall into place. Every worry I'd had that maybe I would one day regret this choice fell away.

My brain had rewritten the past, to the point that a life before surgery just seemed silly. My new normal felt right and natural in a way my original set of genitals never did. It was that peace, and feeling of serene connection, that defined gender euphoria for me and my new vagina.

Reflections: A Bridesmaid on Beauty and Letting Go

Mia Violet

British bisexual author and self-love coach

I saw my expression tense in the floor-to-ceiling mirror as I heard it: 'Do you ladies need help?' The voice of the changing-room attendant bounced down the long corridor. 'No thank you!' I squeaked, holding my pose as if any movement might somehow betray that I felt like an imposter here. I was standing in nothing but my flowery underwear, my dress lying in a crumpled pile where it had dropped off the hanger the second I'd tried to attach it. I took a moment to stare at myself and take stock of what I saw. Endearing little A-cup breasts, long red hair in need of a re-dye, cute Winnie-the-Pooh-esque pouch of a belly folding over the top of my waistband, patches of eczema on my arms from the stress I'd been under, a sleepy face that spoke to how reluctant I'd been to get up this morning. Yep. Here I was. Mia Violet. Trans woman. Author. Bisexual. Anxious. Self-conscious. Shopping for a bridesmaid dress.

There were still a few weeks before the wedding, which I considered a blessing, because as much as I was looking forward to being a bridesmaid for the first time in my life, I only knew three people on the guest list. One of which was my girlfriend, Loretta. The other two were the couple getting married, which included Loretta's mother, a woman who had once told me I was like a daughter to her (a statement that had caused me to cry with delight). As for the rest of the guests? Strangers. But not just any strangers. Cisgender heterosexual strangers. The worst kind of strangers. The type of strangers most likely to misgender me and mistakenly assume I was a man.

I looked at the bridesmaid dress hanging on the back of the door. It was pretty. A soft creamy colour with a low-cut neckline and host to paintings of delicate watercolour flowers. It looked elegantly formal. It also looked expensive. But I could do expensive if it meant I got to be a bridesmaid. Could you imagine? Me. A bridesmaid. Someone who used to drag themselves to weddings in baggy shirts while being secretly jealous of everyone who got to wear gorgeous dresses. Hell yes, I was excited. I'd give my life savings to buy this dress if that's what it would take. Or I would if I had any life savings. Regardless of my worries about being seen as a dude on the day, and my social anxiety about being in a room of unknown faces, I wanted this opportunity. It was a combination of several things I adored: weddings, elaborate dresses, socialising and positive attention. As one of only two bridesmaids, I was banking on some prime attention.

As a former quiet, shy and attention-starved child, I had transitioned into a spotlight-chasing diva. The best type of attention? Gender-affirming attention. I lived for that shit. Having people look at me when I felt attractive and feminine was like being serenaded up to paradise by a chorus of golden, glowing angels, singing a soft song celebrating my divine, goddess-like beauty. But those moments were rare. Most days I felt like I'd crawled out of a sewer pipe. To get to that glowing euphoric state, I'd have to push through any anxiety and dysphoria that day, as well as hope nobody was around to drag me back down to earth with a comment about how masculine my jawline was, or how they couldn't figure out my gender. Those moments always felt like being pushed into an icy pool. A sudden shock that interrupted my every thought.

I knew my gender was real and valid regardless of what I looked like, and regardless of who did or did not respect that I was a woman. I knew that in theory, anyway. On some days it was hard to believe that I could apply such an open and inclusive view of gender to myself. To other people? Sure! Of course! But applying it to myself was sometimes tricky. Because of my appearance, I didn't always feel worthy of explicit gendered titles like 'daughter' or 'girlfriend' or 'bridesmaid'. That extended to clothes too; sometimes an outfit almost felt *too* pretty for me to be seen in. I hated that I felt that way. It felt gross and fuelled by internalised transphobia. Yet it was the truth. I didn't know what it was like to move through the world without being so intensely aware of how you looked and who was watching. So being a bridesmaid at a wedding? It sounded like I'd be more anxiously aware than ever.

Realising I'd been staring at my half-naked body for quite some time, I figured I should actually try the dress on. I grabbed it from the hanger, unzipped the back and tossed it over my head. *Don't rip it, don't rip it, don't rip it.* I contorted and squeezed my body into its shape, desperately trying not to push any part of me too hard against the tight fabric. I fidgeted and shifted before finally: freedom! My head popped free, followed by my arms. I brushed down the dress, an instinctive gesture to iron out any wrinkles, though unnecessary, given how heavy the dress's material was. Right, it was time to check the damage. I brought my gaze up and looked into the mirror. I laughed.

'How is it?' Loretta's voice was muffled, calling to me from the changing room opposite mine, where she'd been trying on her own bridesmaid outfit. I twisted to get a look at the dress from the side and couldn't help but laugh again. Hopping excitedly on the spot, I shouted my answer back: 'It's perfect!' There it was. Those singing angels. Bliss. Thank you, dress.

One month later I was in the guest bedroom of the flat belonging to both Loretta's mother and (soon to be) stepdad. I was staring at my reflection again. I was in the bridesmaid dress, the one that had made me feel graceful and gorgeous. But now all I could see were flaws. Not flaws in the dress – flaws in me. I saw all the little features from my first puberty poking through my face and frame. I didn't look like a woman, or an attractive person by any standards. How the hell did I think I was going to get away with being a bridesmaid? Everyone would know I was a sham as soon as I walked in. A role offered to me out of pity, something I could delude myself into thinking I deserved. This was a terrible idea. I had missed London Pride for this too! Denied myself a day out in the sun with friends so I could feel horrible and have my bizarre body paraded in front of people who would never understand my life, or the time and tears I spent clawing myself here from where I started. I hated this. I didn't want to be here any more.

Throwing myself onto the bed, I closed my eyes and screamed into a pillow. No! I was not going to play this game. Not this time. Not again. These words and cruel thoughts were not mine; they were the lies of gender dysphoria leaking through the cracks of my self-esteem and anxiety. I was feeling vulnerable and scared about the oncoming day, as anybody would be, and that had invited all my old insecurities out to play. Well, bring 'em on!

I rolled off of the bed and got to my feet. Today I was going to be a beautiful bridesmaid. I told myself that was a fact as true as water being wet and pizza being delicious. Yes, it was entirely possible, maybe even likely, that I would get some form of transphobia today while at the wedding. At the very least, a weird look. If that happened, then it happened. I could deal with it. Nay, I *would* deal with it. What I wouldn't do is crawl back into bed and let everybody down. My dysphoria would not win.

I moved to sit in front of my makeshift vanity, a former computer desk that I had commandeered and littered with my cosmetics. Make-up was my favourite form of self-expression. It was how I showed the world my personality, and how I showed myself love and attention. It was time to use all these products to lovingly craft a look for the ceremony, as well as tame my freshly dyed scarlet hair into something that looked less like bloody tumbleweed. I locked eyes with my reflection. Let's do this. 'Suit up, bitch.'

An hour later I was sitting in the back of a car on our way to the town hall for the wedding. I checked my reflection for about the ninety-third time in my trusty clamshell mirror. Cherry-red lipstick. Curled eyelashes. The cutest blush ever applied to a human cheek. A highlight so reflective that it could be seen from space. Yes. I had done well. This was a look to be proud of, something loud and authentically me. We had reached maximum Mia.

We all clambered out of the car into a dingy basement car park that was so at odds with how we were dressed I couldn't help but laugh. We were a four-person wedding entourage dressed in silks and elegant fashion walking through the type of place that was usually reserved as a doomed shortcut for Batman's parents. At least if we got mugged and I went out like Martha Wayne in a mess of bullets and pearls, then nobody could be transphobic to me at the wedding. I would dodge one metaphorical bullet by taking a literal bullet. Ha. Unless the ambulance staff misgendered me and recorded my corpse as male. That would suck. But it would mean I could return and haunt the crap out of them as a vengeful ghost.

Thankfully, we didn't die on our way out of the car park, but we did realise we had arrived quite early. We had about half an hour to kill before we were all set to meet the wedding party. Since we were passing through a spacious (and most importantly) air-conditioned indoor plaza of restaurants, we decided to take a break and sit down. As I often did whenever I was conscious, I pulled out my phone to take some selfies. Tragically the bridesmaid dress did not have pockets, but I had brought an elegant little white purse with me that I'd managed to squeeze my phone and mirror into. If I'd been told I wasn't allowed to bring a purse to the wedding I would have insisted on spending the ceremony with my phone buried in my bouquet. Leave my phone at home? You'll have to kill me first. While snapping selfies I wandered around the plaza in search of the best lighting.

Loretta laughed as I skipped around, stretching my arm out and tilting my body into different poses; this deep into our relationship she was used to me taking selfies at every opportunity. 'My girlfriend, the selfie queen,' she would often teasingly say when my phone came out. That always made me feel good, the girlfriend part especially. For me, taking selfies was like spinning a roulette wheel. I could strike the jackpot or I could lose everything. I never knew who I was going to see looking back. A wonderful perk of having both gender dysphoria and body dysmorphia. Lucky me.

Today was an average day. The selfies were okay, but it was hard to get a proper look at my dress. I wandered over to a window to try to get a look at my reflection instead. In the darkened glass I still couldn't get a good impression, but I liked what little I did see. I took the hem of my dress with one hand and flung it out as I pirouetted from one foot to another. I felt cute. But I knew this was just the warm-up. A growing nervous thought reminded me that soon I'd have a whole lot of eyeballs on me.

Dun-dun-duuuun. The opening notes of *War of the Worlds* reverberated through the town hall corridor as I began my march behind the bride. *Dun-dun-duuuun.* I snorted and tried to get any laugher out of my system before we walked into the hall and everybody saw us. The fact Loretta's mother had chosen the track that heralds the beginning of *The Coming of the Martians* for her bridal march was both baffling and ridiculously on-brand. A few more steps and we were into the room. A wide, open hall with giant bay windows set against nineteenth-century architecture and a ceiling that seemed to rise up for ever. At the front of the room was the wedding officiant and the groom, and along the way were rows and rows of people I'd never met. Eep.

For a frozen moment I took stock of what was happening. I was walking into an ornate stone room filled with staring strangers. Having done my own make-up, I was dressed as a bridesmaid in a pricey dress, and Richard Burton, who'd been dead since before I was born, was loudly warning us all through the sound system that beings from Mars were coming to attack Earth. To top it off, the only people in this room I knew were ones I had originally met when I had a beard and a completely different identity. If I could have told my younger, hairier self that I'd one day be in this moment, I'd have assumed heavy amounts of LSD were involved. Despite the profoundness, I kept my head high and my hands clasping my bouquet as I stepped down the aisle.

The ceremony went by in a flash. I'd wanted to stay in the moment and enjoy it, but I'd been stuck on high alert. The day was going well so far, yes, but I still felt seconds away from a confused look of horror or a harsh bark of laughter. Staying alert made me feel more resilient, like it would somehow sting less if I could see the misgendering coming, but it also disconnected me from any chance of enjoying myself. It was like tiptoeing around on glass. At least we were all now outside, on the grand stone steps of the town hall, taking photos and socialising. As we'd previously been rushed into the ceremony without much chance to say 'Who the hell are you?' I was also being introduced to lots of new faces. Sisters, nieces and the odd nephew made up the bulk of the procession, but there were a few aunts and uncles rounding things out. As expected, all cis, all straight, all... surprisingly polite?

'I look really nice!' I yelped with delight. I wasn't used to being able to stomach photos of me by other people. Normally I needed to take a few dozen selfies from twenty different angles to get a good one. But Loretta's aunt had just snapped one and I liked it. I liked *me*. 'I need more.'

Loretta laughed. Then she realised I wasn't joking. 'Oh. Okay then.' I handed her my phone and skipped over to a stone pillar about four times my height. I leaned against it, trying to channel my inner model and carefree socialite. Yes, behold. It is I. Glamorous bridesmaid, visiting the city from my coastal home. I am deep in thought. Beings as beautiful as myself are always reflecting by large pillars. Later I may drape myself across a sofa while wearing what looks like a net curtain.

'Are you coming?' It was Loretta's stepdad who'd called over to us. He was standing halfway down the steps with his new bride even further ahead of him. The rest of the wedding entourage had already set off for the reception and vanished entirely. I'd just been too busy posing for the last few minutes to even notice their absence. 'Er. Yeah! Okay!' I called over, before looking back to Loretta. 'Quick, one more!' I hissed, snapping into a new pose as she seemed to wrestle with whether to roll her eyes or laugh at how much fun I was having.

At the garden-party reception, my high continued. I strolled around like a princess, sharing stories with other guests and cooing over the youngest members of the party. 'Are they your nails?' I spun around to see a woman about my age gesturing to my hands. 'Yep! All me.' I brought my hand up and wiggled a set of long nails painted a glittery silver. 'Ugh. I'm jealous. I could never get them that long.' I smiled as I bounced over to her and we began chatting about manicures.

Later, while stuffing a choking hazard's worth of mini

sausage rolls in my mouth, something occurred to me. Yep. There it was. Gender euphoria, welcome back. Since posing on the steps back at the town hall, I had ascended to my truest self. Calm, loving, elated, entirely at peace. This feeling was everything. And yet it was everything because it was also nothing. It was normalcy. A sense of rightness that everything was just how it should be. When you've spent your life chafing against people's incorrect assumptions about you, wearing clothes that feel like they could never fit, and moving through the world with an intangible sense of wrongness, then, when everything suddenly feels aligned and comfortable, it's utter bliss. It's like a mix between slipping into a warm bath and hugging your best friend, but times infinity.

I didn't feel the fatigue from all the day's excitement until we were back at the flat. All of us were beat, ready to head immediately to bed. After saying goodnight I returned to my ramshackle vanity. Once I finished removing my make-up, I sat back and looked at my reflection again. All the glamour of the day was gone, either piled on the floor or smeared onto a cleanser-coated face pad. I was back to my most mundane self. But there I was in the mirror again. Mia Violet. Trans woman. Author. Bisexual. Beautiful. Woman.

It wasn't clothes, make-up or titles like bridesmaid, girlfriend or daughter that validated who I was. Nor was it the absence of insults that had sent me on that gender-euphoric high. It was me. For once I had stopped looking at everyone around me to try and predict their opinions or foresee any oncoming judgement. I had let all control of the situation go. I had dropped my guard and allowed myself to just be. To have fun. To play and enjoy being this new version of myself. The version that had released the fear, the guilt, the shame and the jealousy. I didn't need to analyse every situation and prepare myself for a fight. Nobody could take this joy and this truth from me. No matter what anybody else thought or did, I was free. I could always laugh and pose on the steps for photos, I could skip through a park like a princess in a pretty dress, and I could chat about make-up with a new friend. This was my life, my future. I would go to bed now as that cute bridesmaid, and I would wake up tomorrow as her too. No matter what I wore, or said, or did, I would always be her. Always be me.

In the reflection, I saw myself smile.

Life at the Trans-Intersex Intersection

Mari Wrobi

A queer, non-binary and intersex activist currently
living and advocating in Sacramento, California

It all started with one simple question.

'When was your last period?'

I had a few tactics for answering this specific question whenever my doctor asked it. My go-to was relatively straightforward – I would lie. I would usually say something along the lines of, 'It was at the beginning of the month.' This answer was great because it prompted no further questions and we were able to move right along with our appointment. Other days I would pretend that I had just lost track of time. 'I think it was at the beginning of the month, but I'm not quite sure...' This answer seemed believable every once in a while. I mean, it's not like everyone who has a period always remembers when it last started, right? And it didn't technically feel like lying to my doctor when I told her, 'I don't know,' or, 'I don't remember,' either – but deep down, I knew it was. Still, I found that if I rotated answers and used a different one each time, it didn't raise any red flags.

The one answer that I *never* gave her, though, was the truth.

'I've never had my period.'

For years and years prior, I had prayed to any force that would listen to *please not let me get my period*. At the time, I identified as a boy and – despite the fact that people of all genders can have a period – I felt that having my period would completely shift the way I thought about my gender. I had no idea what *actually* caused my lack of periods, but I didn't want to risk it by asking any questions either. I was vaguely worried that if my doctor found out, she might tell me, 'It's okay, you're just a late bloomer!' and that my period would be right around the corner. I was also concerned that there might be some way to 'correct' the mistake of me not having a period, even though I felt validated in my identity exactly as I existed. So I did everything in my power to avoid answering that one simple question.

Everything changed the day I blurted out the truth.

By the time I was twenty years old, I knew two very important things about myself. First, that I was non-binary. Second, that I was intersex.

The journey to figuring out my gender started first. At the age of twelve I learned the word 'transgender' from an episode of *Law & Order*. Even though the episode was shaped by outdated and offensive stereotypes, I immediately felt drawn to the term 'transgender' and intrinsically knew that it was the language I had been searching for. My childhood had been peppered with a few indicators that I felt comfortable, and even preferred, to think of myself as a boy. In almost all of my dreams, I *was* a boy. I dreamed about having girlfriends, about being a dad, and even about being an old man. I strongly preferred to pee standing up, and was confused when my parents consistently tried to get me to sit down. I even remember drawing a picture of myself with a penis as a child – only for my parents to tell me that I didn't have one and to show me how I was *supposed* to draw myself.

At thirteen, I announced to myself – and to everyone around me – that I was a boy.

I grew into a comfortable relationship with myself and my body. The first time I got my hair buzzed, my mom looked at me with a half-smile and said, 'Don't worry, it'll grow back.' But I was so happy with it that I ran my fingers through what was left of my hair for an entire month. Even though my parents were disapproving, I began to shop exclusively in the men's department and would sneak the clothes I wanted into the basket when they were turned the other way. When my parents finally accepted that it wasn't a phase, I began to receive hand-me-downs that affirmed my identity. I also legally changed my name, and everyone in my school and home life called me Adam.

Five years later I was surprised by a second big realisation about my gender – that I didn't feel completely comfortable as a boy. When I first came out, the only trans people who received recognition were those who identified as trans men and trans women. Now I was beginning to see more and more people who identified as non-binary – or as a gender *other* than a man or a woman. I felt the same way about the term 'non-binary' as I initially felt about 'transgender' – and at eighteen years old I once again announced my gender to myself and everyone around me when I came out as non-binary.

It was then that I told my doctor that I'd never had my period.

I blurted out the words, 'Is it normal that I've never had my period?' once my curiosity finally got the best of me. My doctor looked me up and down and decided that we should figure out what was causing my lack of periods. The answer seemed simple at first – I had unusually high levels of testosterone, around the same that someone assigned male at birth would have. Not only that, but my oestrogen levels were essentially post-menopausal. Because of this hormonal variation, my doctor explained that most of my sex characteristics had been 'masculinised'. At first, she diagnosed me with polycystic ovarian syndrome (PCOS) but upon further testing I was re-diagnosed with non-classic congenital adrenal hyperplasia (NCAH).

Though I wasn't fazed by the diagnosis, my doctor told me that I had to begin hormone replacement therapy *immediately* – by taking androgen blockers and oestrogen. As a non-binary person, I wasn't interested in HRT that would conform my body to the gender I was assigned at birth when my body clearly wasn't meant to fit within the binary in the first place. When I let her know that I wasn't interested, her initial suggestion quickly turned into a threat. 'If you don't start hormone replacement therapy now,' she told me, 'you will get cervical cancer. I bet you'll have it in five years. And if you continue to refuse treatment, I can't help you.' I decided then and there that that was the end of our contact. This was not the doctor for me.

What I learned after leaving my doctor's care was more helpful than anything I had learned with her. For instance, congenital adrenal hyperplasia (CAH) is one of the most common intersex variations in the world – yet my doctor never uttered the word 'intersex' during the three years that I had appointments with her. I learned that this type of selective disclosure is unfortunately very common within the intersex community – mostly due to societal and medical stigma, and a lack of comprehensive intersex education even among doctors.

I also learned that the sex binary is often taught to us as a biological reality, when it's not. According to the sex binary, there are two sexes that are determined by one's chromosomes, hormones, external genitalia, internal reproductive anatomy and secondary sex characteristics – male and female. Only sex isn't a perfect binary and male and female aren't the only two options. 'Intersex' is an umbrella term that describes anyone who has sex characteristics that don't fit neatly into either binary sex category. While there are approximately thirty medically recognised intersex variations, it's more accurate to say that there are hundreds of thousands (if not billions) of experiences of sex. That said, sex is just as much of a social construct based on gender norms and expectations as gender is.

What's more is that intersex variations are *extremely common*. Every time I mention that I'm intersex to someone who only has peripheral intersex knowledge, I'm met with comments like, 'Wow, that's so rare! One in a million!' But the actual statistic? About one in fifty. That's 2 per cent of the population – which is the same percentage of the population as redheads, people with green eyes, and twins respectively. Yet because of the lack of comprehensive intersex education, most people believe that intersex variations only include the highly sensationalised genital variations – when they actually include variations in chromosomes, gonads and hormones too.

Connecting with the intersex community allowed me to fully understand and accept the body that I was born with and the identity that was always mine to claim.

While I felt an immediate connection to my trans identity and claimed it quickly after realising that I *was* trans, my intersex identity took a bit more convincing. Soon after I first came out to myself as intersex, I struggled with the feeling that I was an imposter and didn't actually belong in the community – mostly due to all the misinformation about intersex people that I had received over the years and accepted at face value. The more I talked to other intersex people, though, the more I began to hear elements of *my* story in everyone else's – and I slowly began to feel more and more confident to accept that I was intersex too.

I was also able to connect with other people who exist at the intersection of intersex and trans, much to my surprise. On the outside, the intersex community can be oversaturated with stories from cisgender intersex people, as our society finds these stories more palatable. I eventually learned that up to 40 per cent of intersex people identify as trans, though, and these connections were a vital part to my understanding that I could be both without sacrificing one or the other.

Though I didn't know the term at the time, the reason that I felt so comfortable in my body when I didn't have my period was because of the gender euphoria I got from the idea of my body existing naturally outside of the binary. One way that 'gender euphoria' can be defined is as the experience of satisfaction and joy that someone gets when their gender and the way it is externally and internally experienced are congruent. On the other hand, 'gender dysphoria' is the experience of discomfort and distress that someone gets when there is incongruity between their gender and the way it is externally and internally experienced. While a lot of trans people experience *dysphoria* due to puberty, the way that I experienced puberty as an intersex person actually validated the way that I feel about my gender as a non-binary person.

At first I did feel dysphoric. When I was presented with a book about all the changes that my body was *supposed* to go through during puberty, I was met with an unmistakable knot in the pit of my stomach. I thought that it was normal to feel uneasy about the thought of puberty, and I'm sure it is to some extent. But the longer I sat with it, the more I realised that I wasn't uneasy – I was downright *terrified* by the thought of puberty. And as I became more and more aware of my transness, I began to dread what I thought puberty would bring.

But my intersex puberty, as I like to call it, didn't bring most of the changes that I was so afraid of – and as a non-binary person, I was overjoyed with the changes that I actually *did* experience.

The gender euphoria that I got from not having a period was like a wave of relief and comfort that helped me finally feel at peace in my body. Despite the fact that people of all genders can have a period, the highly gendered nature of the way society views the experience and the stereotypical association with womanhood made me feel incredibly othered and invalidated as a non-binary person. Being able to distance myself from this experience as an intersex person, though, while still allowing me to love the other parts of being assigned female at birth helped me appreciate my body and its existence outside of the biological binary.

Another aspect of my intersex puberty that delighted me was the thick body hair that earned me the nickname 'Chewbacca' from my family. While they definitely intended for it to shame and bother me, the moment I realised that I had more body hair than my brother I was *ecstatic*. I constantly had other trans people tell me that they were jealous of my body hair and how well it helped me pass when I presented as a guy. My body hair also enabled me to subvert the expectation that anyone could assume my gender based on my appearance – and the act of wearing a dress with my unshaved legs filled me with a sense of non-binary pride.

Similarly, I had facial hair that was dense and clustered around my chin, jawline and upper lip. Sometimes I would shave, and shaving my face sparked a memory of my dad shaving his face early in the morning and smelling like aftershave for the rest of the day. I never considered that I would be able to shave my face too, and it became a gendered ritual that I never got tired of. Other times, I decided to make my facial hair even darker and more noticeable with mascara so that I could show off the way that my body naturally adorned me with hair. Rather than feeling pressured to shave or hide my body and facial hair, I figured that if my body decided that I should have it, who was I to argue?

My intersex puberty also enabled me to exist in a more androgynous way than I would've been able to otherwise.

For one thing, my voice stayed at a relatively neutral pitch even after puberty. I remember the first time that I came out to a friend as trans and they admitted that they assumed I was a cisgender gay man with a 'gay lisp' because of how androgynous my voice was. I also stayed relatively flat-chested and curveless throughout puberty in a way that allowed me to play with my gender and presentation. Because my body didn't conform to either binary, 'passing' as either gender was easier and I didn't feel dysphoric wearing clothes that were either hyperfeminine or hypermasculine. I felt just as euphoric the day that I was gifted a binder to bind my breasts as I did the day that I was gifted a lacy bra. I didn't feel like I needed to choose one or the other – instead it felt like I had a whole world of opportunity and I could look however I wanted, whenever I wanted.

My intersex puberty has even helped me realise that a lot of the things that I initially believed indicated a trans identity – like when I preferred to pee standing up and when I viewed myself as having a penis – were actually intersex experiences related to the perception of my intersex body. I had no context at the time to describe these distinctly intersex experiences, so I turned to the trans community and was able to find a home within it. The overlap of these two communities within me has taught me that we are not confined by these binaries. We do not need to conform to completely arbitrary ideas and characteristics that the sex and gender binaries have created just because it's what we're 'supposed' to do.

Since settling into my identities as a non-binary person *and* as an intersex person, I have been able to live a more fulfilled and authentic life than I ever would've believed possible when I first learned the word 'transgender' at twelve years old.

While I was initially very uninterested in a medical transition, I eventually decided that I wanted to pursue hormone replacement therapy. I knew right away that my HRT would look very different than it traditionally does but, rather than let the fear of the unknown deter me, I allowed myself the opportunity to make my HRT journey uniquely *me*. I began micro-dosing oestrogen, or taking a lower dose than what is typically provided, in order to retain many of the attributes that I had acquired through my intersex puberty while adding those of oestrogen too. If it weren't for the strong sense of bodily autonomy that I had cultivated growing into my identities, I likely would've avoided HRT indefinitely and thereafter all the positive benefits I have experienced since then.

My understanding and acceptance of my identities has also given me the ability to advocate on behalf of my community. In 2019, I worked alongside interACT: Advocates for Intersex Youth, Equality California, and the American Civil Liberties Union to lobby for SB 201 – a bill in California that sought to delay non-consensual and intersex surgeries on intersex children and infants until they could provide informed consent for themselves. While the bill died in committee in early 2020, being able to discuss my own experience with key decision makers and educate the general public on intersex rights has been an empowering experience that I won't soon forget. I similarly feel confident to advocate for the trans community at my internship at the Gender Health Center, a non-profit in Sacramento that provides free services to trans people in the area, and in my work at the first and only shelter for LGBTQIA+ youth experiencing homelessness in Sacramento. I feel incredibly lucky for the chance to give back to my communities in this way, as they have completely and totally transformed my life.

If it weren't for my intersex identity, I'm not sure where my gender might be. But one thing I know for sure is that my gender can be anything I want it to be.

Gender Affirmation Through Girly Sleepovers

Laura Kate Dale

Growing up pre-transition, sleepovers were one of those formative experiences I never really got to engage in, at least not in the way I had always dreamed about. As a kid I would sometimes sleep at the house of a male friend, or have a friend spend the night at mine, and they were technically sleeping over, but what I wanted out of those experiences often differed from what my friends wanted.

Every time I heard my sister having friends visit, or watched a TV show depicting a girly sleepover, I would be reminded of the same fact over and over: I wasn't seen as a girl, and I wasn't welcome as a part of female friendship groups without caveats.

As a young child, not yet out as a trans woman, most of the friends I had during my formative years were boys. It makes sense: when you're really little, girls think boys are gross, and boys think girls are icky. Tales of cooties and gendered germs encourage division along gendered lines, which are only reinforced by sexist and often homophobic bullying of those who create cross-gender friendships.

Boys who make friends with girls are considered 'gay', or weak, and have to deal with the baggage that comes with that.

And, on top of that, even if you can make friendships across gendered lines, those friendships come with limitations attached. I had a couple of female friends at a few points growing up, but when those friends decided to meet up outside of school together, I was never invited to join them. I was a boy; boys don't take part in social gatherings outside of school, it just isn't done.

As a child, there was a barrier I knew I wasn't allowed to cross. No matter how close a friend I became to the women around me, I was always going to be kept at arm's length for safety. I was always going to be one of their 'guy friends' rather than simply their friend. My gender was a factor, and one I was reminded of any time I tried to make friendships that felt more natural for me.

And even as a teenager, once those barriers began to melt away a little and I started to develop more friendships with women, those boundaries often still existed. The idea of someone seen as a boy sleeping over at a teenage girl's house was just not an acceptable concept. Parental assumptions that any cross-gendered friendship was a gateway to sexual or romantic relationships meant that sleepovers, as they were presented in pop culture, were not on the table for me.

I could see my female friends as part of a group. I could see them at daytime events. I could socialise with them in public. But as soon as it came time to socialise at someone's house, the line was drawn. I wasn't welcome. I wasn't a girl.

Sure, I could have male friends over. We could stay up late eating junk food and watching gross-out-humour movies, but that was sort of where it ended. We had some fun nights, we had some good times, but I always felt I wasn't quite at ease. We never talked about how we were feeling. We never really bonded in that kind of way. We shared a space and shared activities, but something was always a little off. The idea of nights spent cuddled up in blankets together, talking about feelings, connecting emotionally, laughing and being open about ourselves was never really an option. I know it's a silly thing to want, but I grew up really envious of the concept of getting to take part in a stereotypical girly sleepover. I was envious of people who got to be friends with girls without caveats. I was envious I wasn't seen as a girl.

With that said, this is the story of how, through a new hobby that required lots of time and effort, girly sleepovers became a regular part of my life, if a little later for me than for my peers.

When I was in my late teens, in the couple of years prior to my coming out as transgender, one hobby I picked up and got really into was cosplaying, and attending anime and gaming conventions. For the uninitiated, cosplay is basically the concept of creating a costume designed to look like a fictional character from a piece of media, then wearing that costume to an event with other fans of similar pieces of media, many of whom are also dressed up as their favourite characters. It's an often multiple-day opportunity for people with nerdy or geeky interests to find other people who like the same things they do, and socialise en masse. It's an opportunity to spend some time in a setting where everyone has a social safety-net topic, and shared interests are visible at a glance, which for a shy autistic person who struggled to make friends was really appealing. I could spot other people wearing outfits from series I knew, start a conversation, and if things faltered I knew I could ask about the series they were cosplaying from, or how their costume was made.

The first couple of times I went to conventions, the costumes I went along in were pretty simple and easy to put together. Cut-up T-shirts with printed character logos glued onto them, spray-on temporary hair dye, cheap bandages wrapped around limbs, and marker pen drawn directly onto the skin. The outfits were thrown together in a couple of days, and just about got across the general idea of the character, even if they were not particularly accurate or detailed. I had a couple of female friends who I would go to conventions with, and we would usually just head up to and back from the event in a single, very lengthy day, but the more we attended events, the more we enjoyed our time there, and the more ambitious our ideas for costumes became.

No longer were we happy with costumes thrown together from existing bits of clothing. Sewing machines were pulled out to sew custom pieces from patterns. Fabric shops were scoured together for the perfect pieces of material. We started to learn how to make props out of plastics, foam, card and paint. Our costumes became more elaborate and we didn't want to just attend for a single day each time. We wanted to be there all weekend, with a full selection of different outfits to wear. It was becoming an event our life revolved around a couple of times per year.

The first time I remember having a gender-affirming sleepover with female friends took place a little while before I actually came out as trans, and is one of those events I look back on as a first in experiencing what my life would one day become. It was one of my first times feeling validated as part of a female friendship, and an early taste of gender euphoria, even if that fact was only clear in hindsight.

It was the week before MCM London Comic Con, the UK's biggest nerdy convention in terms of pure numbers of people attending, and none of us had finished our costumes. One of my friends had a prop scythe that still needed several coats of paint, I had a wig that still needed styling, and one of our friends still needed to adjust the fit on several items of clothing. We all knew we were going to need a few very late nights to get ready, so I asked my parents if this pair of friends could sleep over the night before the convention. I made the argument that we had a lot of creative craft work that needed doing on a deadline, and that the visit was exclusively about us working together and helping each other stay motivated to finish our work. I showed them the costume parts I had already made, explained what still needed making, and they said I was welcome to have them both stay over.

We ended up staying awake all night that night, and I remember very clearly how different the energy of the night felt from any time I'd had male friends sleep over my house. It was night and day. We watched romantic comedy anime together, talked, laughed and worked on craft projects right through the night. At around 2 a.m. we all went to the nearby supermarket in our pyjamas together to grab snacks for the long day ahead. We hugged, we opened up and we had more fun than I think I had ever had with female friends before. Something about the friendship felt different and brought out a side of me that had never come out around the male friends I had grown up with.

It was an eye-opening experience. I finally felt like I had been let into a female friendship, and I felt at home in a way I never really had before. This was what I wanted my friendships with others to be. This was who I wanted to be in friendships. I couldn't put a name to the feeling at the time, but I wanted whatever was happening to be a part of my life.

The rest of that weekend honestly went much the same as that first sleepover night before the convention. We shared a pretty tiny hotel room at the convention to save money as broke students, all sleeping wedged up in a single double bed, and our evenings were spent laughing, fixing up our costumes and having fun in a way that felt really validating. I think the core of what made that weekend so memorable was simply that I was getting to spend time with my female friends without being expected to leave at a certain point in the night. I wasn't being pushed out of the fun, left on the outskirts, because of the genitals I was born with. I was allowed to be a part of the friendship without caveats.

As fun as that weekend was, looking back on it, it's pretty clear to me in hindsight that it included one of the first instances of me testing the waters that would eventually lead to me coming out as a trans woman. On the second night of the convention, my friends and I went back to our hotel room to get changed into more comfortable outfits to socialise in for the rest of the evening. This involved my friends taking time to redo their hair and make-up and, totally just as a silly joke, I asked if they wanted to mess around doing my hair and make-up too. You know, just as a funny joke, to see how pretty they could make me look.

It's one of the first times I remember trying to engage with female presentation around friends, and seeking help with how best to look my most feminine. I still have a photograph of myself that night. It's the first picture I have of myself trying to look feminine deliberately, but it was certainly not the last. Sure, it was presented to those friends as a joke, not to be taken seriously, but it was the first of many such 'only joking' experiences on the road to me finally talking about how I'd spent a long time feeling.

While that particular friendship group didn't last until I was properly out as trans, I did continue attending conventions, and made a new group of friends who I attend all my conventions with now. The group is largely women, with a couple of non-binary and transmasc friends in the group too, but meeting that group allowed non-masculine sleepovers to become a much more regular ongoing part of my life going forwards. The fact that I get to take part in them now out as a woman is all the better.

A decade on from meeting this group of friends, I now attend conventions with them for full weekends at least twice per year, but also every few months have sleepovers with them where we stay up late playing Dungeons & Dragons, laughing at memes, and catch up with each other on how life is treating everyone.

The first few times I went to conventions with this group of friends, I was barely out of the closet as trans. I'd had no medical interventions, I was still working out how to present myself as female, I was awkward, and I didn't always know what I was doing. They didn't care. From day one they treated me as a woman, and made me feel accepted and included in our weekends spent together.

I may not have been able to be a part of girly sleepovers as a child or teenager, but as a woman in my late twenties they're a highlight of my social calendar.

Clippers and Clarity: Cutting My Own Hair for the First Time

Parker Armando Deckard

Twenty-two, Filipino-American non-binary trans man

My family has always been preoccupied with appearances. I'm not sure when it started or if it was there to begin with, but there has always been this obsession with how we act, how we talk, how we dress and present. It is all seen as a reflection of our family, and with the children it is seen as a reflection of the way our parents raised and taught us. In a way it makes sense, with my dad being born in the United States and my mother emigrating from the Philippines when they got married. My father grew up in poverty with a father in the military who, despite his best efforts, was often away from home, working to provide everything he could for his family. My mother faced her own challenges as a new immigrant in the United States, forced to experience the particular brand of racism and discrimination that came with that journey. My father works as a doctor and my mother works as a nurse, and everything they do is to create a good life for their family.

My parents have worked extremely hard to get where they are today, and they reiterate over and over that they simply want the best for their kids (even if at times, it feels like we were meant to simply reflect our parents).

As generation 1.5 in a Filipino-American family, we're an odd group of kids. We know our lives are very different from the way our parents grew up, but we don't fit into the stereotypical image of an American family. As a result, we have a certain way we are expected to act. We always have to keep up appearances, keep a certain pristine image so we have the best chances in life.

The image they want us to fit, however, is very much the image of the Christian American, and with that role comes many people we are expected to be. In church we were expected to play the part of the quiet, devout Christian, reading the Bible and scripture, praying the rosary every day, and going to weekly Mass. In school it was the part of the devoted student, studying and taking notes, always listening to teachers, asking pertinent questions, but keeping quiet and keeping out of trouble. At home it was the part of the obedient child, who listened diligently, never spoke out of turn, and followed the example of the parents.

As we were growing up, my parents expressed that they knew that all of us would be different to some degree as we got older, and that these differences didn't have a bearing on how they loved us. This statement has never changed, but it has been put into context over the years for me. I gave my parents a startling revelation when I started college. They had always expected each of their children to be different, but they never expected their eldest daughter to end up being a bisexual, non-binary trans man. It was not a discovery that was welcomed by my parents. As I continue to live at home, I never feel quite safe enough to talk to them about it without bursting into tears or freezing where I stand. It caused quite a stir in the house, as they gradually found out over the years that their firstborn was nothing that they had ever planned for.

When I first came out to my mother as bisexual, she asked if I was cheating on my partner. My father asked if he should out me to my college roommate's parents because my bisexuality made me a seemingly 'dangerous' roommate. When I was stressing over being a trans person in a conservative Christian household and I couldn't tell my father what was bothering me, he refused to speak to me until I told him what was wrong. When I came out to my mother as trans, she said that neither of them would ever accept it, and that I knew they couldn't. After my mother had gone that night to tell my father, I was left with the knowledge that my parents would never accept me, that they would love the me they had raised but not the me that I had become. It was something I had known for a long time but had never quite accepted until that moment. The hug I received from my father the following morning didn't do much to quell the feelings inside. As I live and interact with them each day, I know they haven't accepted that they can't change who I am, though I'm unsure if they'll continue to blame that fact on a godless college education corrupting my mind.

I won't say I never tried to follow the image they wanted of me. I spent years trying to be the Christian daughter who stayed within the Church, to be everything they always wanted, because the alternative terrified me. For years I found that it was easier to follow rather than stand out. It was easier to stay quiet rather than question Church hypocrisy. It was easier to blend in rather than speak against violent homophobia from a Catholic teacher. It was easier to conform than to openly express myself, whether that be with my love, my dress or expression.

For a long time a lot of this conformity was tied to my hair. For years others told me how they loved my hair and how long and beautiful it was. For as long as I can remember, my mother was always putting it up, brushing it back tightly and putting it in hairdos that earned the 'ooohs' and 'aaahs' of onlookers, but earned me a headful of hairspray and a headache. It was something for others to gawk and stare at, something to mark me as feminine, as 'correct'. For me, it was something to be tied back, put away, a reminder of something I wasn't getting quite right but went along with despite the discomfort. For the longest time, my hair was something I hated. This started to change during high school. At some point I had mentioned wanting to get my hair cut short, and a classmate had said that I shouldn't because I would end up looking like a boy. While I didn't voice it at the time, I didn't object to the idea of being seen as a boy. It was something that had never crossed my mind before. I had never thought I could be anything other than what I was told. But the more I thought about it, the more I found that I wouldn't mind it, how it might feel more comfortable. I had never disliked being a girl, but it always felt like a tight sweater on a warm day: wearable, possibly fashionable, but overall uncomfortable. The idea of looking different and being different, of feeling comfortable for once in my life, was something I had never considered before. The uncertainty the thought brought threw my mind in a tailspin. And once I started questioning, it became a lot less easy to live in the role I'd been assigned.

In a house that controlled so much of my life, with a family that dictated so much for me, I felt stifled: not quite unable to breathe, but not taking in full breaths either, unable to fully fill my lungs with air. I would look in the mirror as I tied back my hair and wish I didn't have to deal with the tangles and fretting it brought upon me. Every day was full of countless thoughts of ripping the tresses out of my head, pulling at them like weeds until I was left with nothing but an aching scalp. I came pretty close to doing so on some bad nights. It took a while, but eventually I realised that I didn't have to live like that. It wasn't a sudden realisation or one single moment or instance. It was the slow entertaining of the idea that made me realise it. The idea of doing it myself had floated in my mind for a long time, and the thought of finally being free of my hair was nothing short of a dream come true.

The first time I cut my own hair was during my junior

year of college. I had spent a year growing it out from an unfortunate bob of bleach-fried hair, and begging to get a haircut from my dad. When I showed him pictures of the type of short undercut I'd like, I was always met with the same statements: how I would look like a lesbian, how I would attract women with short hair, how I would look ugly with it, and how I simply looked 'better' and 'right' with the hair I currently had. It's difficult to live with a parent you love and care for deeply, who is supposed to love you back unconditionally, and know that they see some part of you as wrong. I never took the words themselves to heart, but knowing that he felt something was inherently wrong with the way I wanted to be caused a hurt to settle deep in my chest. I'd like to think that this stage in my expression was another stride towards digging that hurt out from inside me.

Going to college and being able to live on campus for a year was the first step towards undoing that hurt. It's only after being given that space that I grew into my own. College was the first time that I truly felt like I was a person. I felt enough confidence to try to live. And so I kept trying. I tried acting, I went to an open-mic night and sang my heart out, I took a creative-writing class and started writing in earnest, and I even joined an a capella group for a while. I came out to people and started using my chosen name during classes, even when sending professors emails about the rosters made my hands shake with nerves. I had a group of friends for the first time in my life, and they cared for me.

Everything was frightening and new and uncertain, but I found people who saw me for me. I found people who didn't want the image I had been raised to project: they preferred the authentic version of me. I found people who wanted to see Parker, and all the eccentricities he had. It was with these people that I realised I didn't fit neatly within the Western gender binary, and the ambiguity of my gender was something to embrace rather than shove into one box or another. It was with these people that I came into my own, and I embraced being trans and expressing myself in the joy of floral print, painted denim and combat boots.

After all this time, I've come to realise that no one can define my identity but me. No one can revoke my 'trans card', and anyone who tries is not worth my energy. It is true that I have never stopped caring about what others think of the way I look or the way I present. I'm not sure anyone truly stops caring what others think; some just get better at tuning out those particularly loud thoughts. I've made some peace with the fact that I don't look like the 'traditional' trans person, because I'm a gender non-conforming, non-binary trans person of colour. I love skirts and dresses, I love nail polish and poetry and pink, but I align myself as masculine. I know I'll never pass; I know I'll never look or act how many believe I should. However, I've stopped categorising parts of myself as 'correct' or 'incorrect'. It's been harmful for me to think of any part of me as 'wrong', for simply existing as it is. There is no singular right way to exist as a living being.

So as long as my body is safe and healthy and alive, I can try to be happy in my own skin.

It's only been within the last year or so that I've tried to stop caring about whether the way I look or act is 'correct'. But, as I stood in my friend's dorm room, staring at the mirror with a hunk of hair clenched in one hand and hair shears in the other, I remember feeling fear. I felt that visceral fear of being wrong, of the retribution that would come if I continued on with the act of even daring to deviate from the path I was supposedly destined to take. I could have stood there for hours, shaking, with the scissors in my hand, tears barely contained from falling down my face. But I didn't. I ended up working the scissors through the thick bunch of hair, dropping it into the waiting garbage bin. As I watched it fall, dread flooded the pit of my stomach. Staring at the jagged edge of the fresh cut, I was in shock at what I had done. I knew that this small act went against everything I had been taught. I could have collapsed on the floor and cried. I think the only reason I continued was because of my friends.

I didn't take this first step on my own. The catalyst for so many of the good things I did for myself was the sweet freedom of having friends who affirmed me and offered support at every turn. They were there when I bleached my hair and dyed it blue, and they were there when it faded to green. They were there when I bought the cheapest pair of hair scissors I could find, and they were there when I stuck gum in my hair to give my parents an excuse for the sudden chop. They were there to even out the back of my haircut when I couldn't see, and they were there to take countless selfies with me as I admired my new bob. They reassured me as I was on the verge of tears, and hyped me up as I ran my hands through my finished haircut. They were as much a part of the experience as I was, and they were still supportive every time I decided to cut my hair in the next two years.

That's not to say it's ever gotten easier. There's a reason most people go to a barber or hair salon rather than trying to do it themselves. Cutting hair on your own is never an easy task, no matter how many times you do it. And the ridicule I got afterwards from my family wasn't easy to deal with either, especially when they pointed out the obvious mistakes I had made when doing it myself. But the freedom that cutting my hair brought is something I hold dear. No one could control it but me, and it's something I won't ever give up.

I bought a pair of hair clippers this summer. It's amazing what isolation for weeks on end can do to a person, especially when they're trying to graduate college at the same time. But a lack of care for what others thought came with the isolation as well, especially when I found out I would be seeing no one but my family for three months. Maybe that's what pushed me to drop the hair clippers in my shopping cart as I went to do a grocery run for my family and pick up medication. I remember smuggling them upstairs under my hoodie, hiding them away in my backpack as soon as I made it safely to my room. They sat tucked away in the box for longer than

I would like to admit. I was worn down from constant deadlines and the most stressful final semester I had ever had. It had left me stretched far too thin and unwilling to take on the added stress of a potentially damning quarantine haircut. But after a digital graduation, I needed something to lighten my mood and spirits. I was ready.

I remember that night a bit clearer. It was around ten o'clock. By that point most things had quietened down, the non-night owls of the family had gone to bed, and those who weren't asleep were too immersed in video games to notice anything. I remember getting set up in the bathroom, watching and rewatching the YouTube tutorials I'd deemed most helpful so I wouldn't do irreparable damage to my hair and end up shaving my whole head as a result. I remember putting on *Star Wars* as I started and barely being able to hear the dialogue over the sound of the clippers buzzing in my ears, but the familiarity was enough to calm my shaking hands before I got to work. And just like that, I was shaving away months of stress that had built up on my head, seeing it give way to a clean buzz of an undercut and a clear head. I'm not entirely sure how long it took. Thirty minutes? An hour? Maybe two? I suppose I'll never know.

What I do know is that by the time I was done, I was left feeling oddly calm. Not floored, not out of breath with anxiety and nerves that were close to bubbling over and drowning me. There was none of that. I just felt happy. Overheated from the overworked clippers, and tired from staying up late, but happy. There's something about running my fingers through newly cut hair, feeling the buzzed fuzz at the nape of my neck, that gives me so much joy. And I have my newfound joy with these clippers, in doing this for myself. They're comfort and calm and clarity wrapped up in numbered guards and combs. They've allowed me to reclaim part of myself, to find happiness in my hair. And no matter what the world throws at me, I know I wouldn't trade my new haircut for anything.

The Tipping Point: Getting Correctly Gendered Without Making an Effort

Laura Kate Dale

When I was early on in transition, back before I was living full time as female or had started on hormones, I made a very focused effort in the way I presented myself when going out into the world to ensure I would be properly read as female by strangers.

I was aware that I was tall, I had creeping facial hair by the end of the day, and I had a lot of learned masculine behaviours to unlearn if I wanted to be perceived by the wider world as female. So, every day I had a careful routine and I followed it for several years. I wanted to feel feminine and I wanted to avoid being seen as male, so I stuck to it.

Every few days, I would manually and slowly pluck all of my facial hair with a pair of tweezers and a mirror, over the course of multiple hours. I would then apply foundation, hoping it would cover any shadow that remained, and put on a scarf, no matter the weather, to hide my huge and pointy Adam's apple.

I would always go out with a tight, fitted top over a stuffed bra to make it look like I had breasts, and wear a dress or a skirt, something considered societally gendered as female, to really hit the message home.

It wasn't always comfortable. There were days I didn't have it in me to sit plucking my face painfully for hours. There were days it was sweltering and I didn't want a scarf on. There were days I just wanted to wear jeans or trousers, rather than needing to make sure my legs were properly shaved to wear a dress with. But I did it, day in and day out, because I wanted to feel valid as a woman, and I wanted the world to see me as the woman I saw in myself.

It was part seeking external validation, part combating dysphoria, and part keeping myself safe. If I was read as female, activities like using a public bathroom became safer, so it was important I give as many clues as possible to point people to that conclusion.

When I first committed to living without exception as a trans woman, I was working a bland and forgettable retail job, stacking shelves, serving customers and working on the checkout. I kept up the routine of daily effort I felt was needed for the world to see me as female. My ability to safely navigate employment and be accepted by my co-workers was dependent on my ability to quickly demonstrate to everyone at work that I was female, and this was a serious thing, not some kind of joke. I would sometimes pluck my face at 3 a.m., ready for a 6 a.m. start at work. I took every effort to be seen as female, based on my outward gender expression.

And, unsurprisingly, it worked. I made an effort to gender-code myself as much as possible, and even if people didn't always actually believe I was female, they could at the very least see I was trying to put that version of myself into the world. I got gendered as female because it was clear I wanted to be seen as female.

But I had a fear, and it was one that persisted for a great many years during my journey as a trans woman. I feared that if I ever missed a day of keeping up these outward-facing appearances, my identity as female would fall away with it. I feared being defaulted to male if a single bit of facial hair broke through. I feared that the world would stop seeing me for who I was if I didn't constantly work at broadcasting my identity outwards.

Not long after coming out full time as a woman, I was lucky enough to be able to move out of that customer-facing retail job and start working from home as a writer. Now, with a supportive partner at the time, and a job that didn't require me to be publicly facing presentable several days a week, I gradually relaxed a little on the efforts I made with my presentation.

So what if I had a bit of facial hair showing on a work day? If I wasn't planning to go out, then it shouldn't really make much difference. Who needs to shave their legs and wear a skirt when working from home? When it's just me in the house, do I really need a bra on all day? Probably not. It was okay to sacrifice some of that outward effort to get a little more of my day for myself, and a little additional relaxation and comfort.

I would still very much make an effort with my appearance if I knew I was going out on a date, or was travelling for work, or was going to go somewhere I might need to access public toilets safely, but day to day, I began to cut myself a little slack on my appearance.

My body is a female body, regardless of whether it gets a bit hairy, or if I'm wearing baggy clothing that isn't explicitly gendered. I started to feel more at peace with my body being what it was, even if I didn't necessarily trust the world around me to view it as a validly female body.

Over the years that followed, in which time I started on hormones and got more experience with my voice and how I carried myself, I started to get more confident about heading into the world in little ways, here and there.

I would go to the shops, not making any particular effort to gender myself as stereotypically feminine to the outside world, little by little less scared of the idea of being misgendered. If someone called me 'sir', that wouldn't be fun, for sure, but I knew I was female, and someone calling me a man wouldn't change that fact. I never went into those days with the assumption I would be correctly gendered; I went in assuming the worst, but knowing that if the worst that happened was someone called me a man, I would come out of that situation okay. I tended to avoid changing rooms or bathrooms, but I would give myself the gift of days where I didn't stress about fighting the body I happened to have.

I can't pinpoint the exact day, because the first few times this happened I wrote them off as accidents or happy surprises, but there was definitely a moment around eighteen months into being on hormones where the way the average stranger perceived me flipped almost overnight, and the experience was one of the most gender-affirming and euphoric aspects of my whole transition.

To put it simply, at some point around a year and a half into being on hormones, I started getting gendered as female by strangers the vast majority of the time, regardless of if I had made an effort to gender-code my presentation or not.

Now, getting gendered as female wasn't a new experience to me in and of itself. I'd spent years making an active effort to be seen as female, introducing myself to people with a feminine name, and going out of my way to push for being gendered correctly. But this was different. I would go to the local supermarket or corner shop with a little facial hair poking through, tracksuit bottoms and a baggy formless shirt, and get greeted as 'miss'.

Now, at the time, that level of acknowledgement as female felt life-changing. It felt like some inherent aspect of myself, deep inside, had suddenly bubbled to the surface. The fact I was a woman was clear for the world to see, even on the days I thought I wasn't doing enough to hide the testosterone trying to break out of me. It felt like something had changed, and suddenly the world could see me for who I was.

Looking back, I can guess at some of the changes around that time that might have contributed to this. I had been practising raising my vocal tone, and perhaps

I suddenly hit the vocal sweet spot that most people default to identifying as female range. Maybe I'd seen some fat redistribution, and my face had changed shape a little. Maybe I just noticed a couple of people gender me correctly while in baggy outfits, got more confident, and got gendered correctly more often because I stopped trying to hide my more feminine behaviours when in lazy mode. It's impossible to know what actually changed, but honestly I didn't need to know the reason, I just knew it was happening, and I was delighted.

When you're first coming out as trans, at least here in the UK, so much of whether you're taken seriously is how well you outwardly present a performance of traditional gendered norms. The first time my mum came to one of my counselling sessions where I was presenting as female, she described how all she could see was her son in a dress. I still had certain features hormones were years away from changing, and as such she struggled to see me as female. Before my first trips to the gender identity clinic, I was warned by fellow trans people that, if I wanted to get prescribed hormones and move through the gatekeeping hoops, I had better turn up to every appointment in my most feminine-coded outfit possible. Fellow trans women had been accused in the past of not really wanting to transition, because for safety or comfort they attended appointments in jeans and a hoodie, with short hair. Cis women are allowed to dress that way and are not seen as less valid as women – it's a core tenet of modern feminism – but if you turn up to a trans healthcare appointment that way, you're clearly not woman enough to get medical help.

When working in that retail job I mentioned earlier, I got told off for sitting wrong while having lunch in the break room. If I didn't sit in a more feminine way, it would be my own fault if my fellow staff didn't treat me as female.

And it's under that context, of constantly having my identity graded on how well I performed traditional gendered presentation, that getting read as female in a big baggy hoodie, comfy trousers, with a pointy Adam's apple on show and some facial hair poking through was so validating.

Whatever the cause, I had reached a point in my life where, even if I was making no effort at all to project who I was, my identity was starting to shine through to the world. I could be lazy, I could be unpolished, and I could still be a woman in those moments.

It was the first time I felt like I was living truly as female. I stopped writing off my lazy days as in some way cheating. Every day I was Laura, and the world was finally starting to see that.

Punks Against Gender Conformity: Being Agender in the Punk Scene

Koda Strider

Twenty-one, neurodivergent, agender, Californian

I was seventeen years old when I first looked in the mirror and felt happy with my reflection. I had just come back from the barber's, where I got the right side of my head shaved; I put on a boy's T-shirt with a black-and-purple flannel top over it, donned purple lipstick and spiky jewellery, and finally saw a genuine smile looking back at me in the mirror. I was feeling a joy I'd never felt before that moment. The exact explanation for that joy eluded me. That is until later that day when my grandmother accidentally referred to me as a 'young man' and then I realised, *Oh, it's a gender thing.*

At the time, I was orphaned and living with my old-fashioned grandmother, and I had no support system outside of the internet. I only had one friend to share these gender feelings with – and she lived on the other side of the country. To help me figure out those feelings, and just to share with me some music she loved, she introduced me to the punk band Against Me!, which has a trans woman as a lead singer. I was very inspired by their music, aesthetics and songs, which combined feelings of frustration at gender dysphoria with general punk protest energy. I wasn't entirely sure if I wanted to be seen as a man or possibly more neutral, so I decided to start experimenting. Since my appearance was what started those feelings, I began my transition there.

Before all this self-exploration fashion-wise, I wore simple women's clothing and cared about comfort over style. My whole wardrobe consisted of floral dresses, tank tops and shorts meant to show off my feminine features. I had tried to break away from that style once before, when I was sixteen, dressing up in a black dress, fishnet stockings and a long purple wig. That outfit made me happier than my other clothes, but it came at a time where I was in denial that I could be anything but feminine. My goal then was simply to look sexy, as I had a very warped view of myself at the time and thought that even at that age my job was to look sexually appealing. My family rejected that phase and forced me to be more basic and modest in the way I dressed, and I was quick to give that style up, even though it did give me a strange hint of confidence. But now that I didn't need parental approval for how I looked, I felt free, and the first thing I wanted to do was get a new wardrobe filled with androgynous or masculine clothing.

With punk music as the soundtrack in this coming-of-age story, I ventured to thrift stores in search of myself.

I shopped in the men's section for the first time, which, strangely enough, made me feel euphoric just from that fact, a feeling that just barely overpowered the anxiety of being seen as female and shopping in the 'wrong' section. I swallowed my fear, avoided everyone's gazes, and simply shopped for whatever I wanted to wear. I got dark flannels, black T-shirts, ripped jeans, shorts covered in chains, belts with spikes on them. With each alternative-styled piece of clothing I added to my wardrobe, I felt more and more of this euphoric feeling.

At this point I also started testing out changes like a new name and new sets of pronouns. My small group of friends online were very supportive and called me by the new name I had picked for myself. When they started using he/him pronouns and masculine titles for me, it felt more right than she/her and feminine titles, but it still didn't feel like me. I searched around online and discovered non-binary people who went by they/them, and when I tried out those pronouns it felt the same as trying on the new clothes in my wardrobe: euphoric. Now I had a name and set of pronouns I was happy with, and each time someone used them I felt that surge of glee again and again. While my family would never accept these changes, I started going by my new name at work, and even though I knew my co-workers still saw me as a girl, I was overjoyed to work in an environment where I could be a little more myself.

The first effects of my newfound confidence were noticeable immediately. I was holding myself differently; I had a wardrobe full of outfits I felt comfortable wearing; I was actually eager to wake up each day and get dressed, since I knew I'd love how I looked. Even my camera roll could see the effects, as I started to take more pictures of myself. There's one photo that brings a smile to my face every time I see it, where I had just returned from a day of thrift shopping and I'm in the kitchen of my grandmother's house wearing my purple flannel and a hat covered in spikes, and I'm hugging myself with glee, since I felt happier in that moment than I had in practically my whole life. I've struggled with getting along with myself, as I've always hated how I looked and acted. But that day, in that moment, I felt such a rush of self-love it had me bouncing off the walls, grinning wider than I had in years, taking selfie after selfie to forever capture the moment where I started to love myself.

The other part of punk fashion that got me hooked was the way traditionally feminine clothing turned unisex. I could wear a crop top, short shorts, fishnet stockings, lipstick, eyeshadow, eyeliner, nail polish, necklaces and earrings and still not feel like a girl at all because of the inherent androgyny that punk carries with it. Suddenly, where I had previously felt awkward about female-coded clothing, when it was black and covered in spikes I felt a lot less uncomfortable about it. I grew up with a wardrobe that consisted of only pink clothing, so that was what I was used to, yet it still felt unfamiliar to me after all those years. So while changing to darker clothes was a new experience, I immediately felt comfortable wearing them due to the completely different connotations black clothes hold. In these new outfits I didn't feel feminine or masculine. I felt like someone else entirely: myself.

As I experimented with clothing, accessories and hairstyles, I was also testing the waters of being a gender aside from female. When I first began this journey by feeling euphoria at being called a 'young man', I thought the obvious answer was that I was a transgender man. But as my online friends started calling me by he/him pronouns and masculine titles like 'man' and 'mister', I quickly realised that that side of the binary didn't feel like *me* either.

I was being very introspective at the time, trying to truly learn who I was and who I wanted to be. As a result I discovered that I am non-binary, specifically agender (which means a complete lack of gender), and that the euphoria from being perceived as a man was only due to my desperation to not be seen as a girl. So while being mistaken as male by strangers feels nice, I know who I am, and that who I am is neither male nor female.

Now I had a word to describe myself, what next? Well, I severed the first and last few letters of my name to create a new, unique, androgynous-sounding name for myself. I officially came out at work and to my friends, as well as making public posts about it on social media. I became a proud member of the trans community.

Of course, those steps were met with varying reactions. My friends were very supportive; my co-workers didn't use my pronouns but did put my new name on my name tag; my family refused all of it and still chastised me for 'trying to look like a boy'. But what mattered most to me is that I felt so much more comfortable in my own skin now that I had a better idea of who I was. Now I had a name, set of pronouns, and a term for my identity, all of which gave me that feeling of euphoria. I was a baby punk, a newly hatched trans person, and I had a wardrobe full of spikes and chains to match.

The self-esteem I got from wearing those types of clothes was otherworldly. I didn't feel the need to hide behind long hair and hoodies any more. I was more than happy to show my skin, despite my myriad of insecurities. I felt attractive for the first time – that alone changed my life. As I started valuing myself more, I stopped settling in friendships and relationships, I stopped blaming myself for everything bad that happened to me, and I held my head high with a smile on my painted black lips every time I walked around.

I even had the confidence to take my life into my own hands and make something beautiful out of it. As I was approaching my eighteenth birthday I could see signs all pointing to the inevitability that I would be kicked out of my living situation, since my extended family believed they had no obligation to provide for me once I reached that milestone. So I took control of the situation. On that fateful July day, with my heart pounding and the clock ticking towards an end where I would end up on the streets, I spent every waking moment working towards getting out of there. I got my ID, my GED (an alternative qualification to the US high-school diploma, showing 'general equivalency development') and a ticket to California, where my best friend lived.

I left behind my job where I was about to be promoted, my entire family, the one real-life friend I had, and I risked it all to take that leap of faith. It was a large sacrifice, but was very worth it. I got the chance to start my life over with a blank slate, where nobody around me knew my deadname or how I used to look. Though getting on my feet in a brand-new place took a lot of effort, being seen as the real me by people who didn't know my past was an amazing and euphoric feeling I wouldn't trade for the world.

In this new life I started building for myself, I had the courage to branch out and meet new people. Those people introduced me to the punk scene in real life, so I no longer had to rely on YouTube videos, illegally downloaded songs and thrift shops to nourish this part of myself.

It started only weeks after my big move, when I went to an Against Me! concert. My friend and I had balcony tickets at the Fonda Theatre in Los Angeles. The show was like nothing I've ever seen before; this was my first concert seeing a punk band. This was also my first time being surrounded by LGBTQIA+ people and punks of colour, seeing anarchists with green mohawks, activists in leather jackets covered in patches, misfits brought together. We all had our fists in the air as we screamed the lyrics to each song until our voices were hoarse; we cheered when someone threw a transgender flag on stage and the singer, Laura Jane Grace, hung it over an amp. The audience bonded in shared anger as we sang together about oppression, gender dysphoria and bigotry. We found strength and unity in the shared experience of being outcasts within our respective communities. It was like this special part of the world carved out exclusively for us, so we could all have a space where we finally belonged. I left that concert feeling more alive than I ever had before, and with new inspiration from the way everyone was dressed however the hell they wanted to.

After that night, I continued to chase the high I experienced from it. I sought out more concerts, underground shows, local punk bands, drag shows and artist alleys. These were events where I felt completely unafraid to be myself, and entirely and utterly euphoric.

I believe that the reason misfits all feel free in the punk scene is because punk itself is all about breaking down tradition and anything else that holds us back from being our truest, happiest selves. It's about dismantling establishments that oppress us. This means something different to everybody. But no matter how that translates to you and your personal struggles, the fight is what we can all relate to. So when I raise my fist against gender norms and a hetero- and cis-normative society, I'm standing beside someone raising their fist against the patriarchy, someone else who's fighting against racial inequality and police brutality, and another person who's screaming in the face of ableist policies. And beyond our individual battles, we fight for each other. Punk, as a community, stands against oppression, and lifts each other up to do so. So when surrounded by each other, everyone in the scene gets to be themselves in a pure, raw form, since nothing is holding them back in that time and space.

It's a sight to behold, really. The blood, sweat and tears we all shed together, the combined power of our shrieks and pain and passion – to me it's the feeling of being alive. It feels like crowdsurfing, where you just lean back and let the mass of people lift you up and carry you forward as far as you can go. We support each other, and only exclude those who mean to bring us down, like bigots. In action, we are truly a force to be reckoned with.

These events were also the most accepting places I'd ever been to. Where else would you find a place surrounded by graffitied walls and pride flags, housing dozens of people wearing whatever the hell they wanted, passing out pronoun pins and selling handcrafted items expressing anti-fascist pro-queer agendas? I saw my first drag show at an underground concert that featured ear-splitting music presented by someone wearing a beard on one side of their face and make-up on the other. I threw every dollar I had at these performers, since they meant the world to me. They showed me that, despite what my assigned family had taught me, there was a place in this world where I could fit in, where I could feel like I belonged. They inspired me to be myself and love who I want. They helped me see that I'm allowed to be happy being me. The confidence of other punks is certainly contagious, and as an introvert it says a lot that my favourite place to be is any type of punk show. The energy in the air is always electrifying, and I leave every event with my cheeks sore from smiling and my voice lost from screaming.

These people being unabashedly themselves inspired me to do the same, and figure out exactly who I was and what I wanted. Now I know how I can be 'feminine' or 'masculine' while still feeling like I'm presenting as neither a male or a female. I learned so much about self-expression from this community, which was more than happy to help out a newcomer. The punk scene in general is so anti-conservative and pro-'be whoever you are, just don't hurt anybody' that I feel way more comfortable meeting new people within that community than I do with any 'normal' person, because there's a much higher chance they'll accept me and use my name and pronouns. The punk scene is so interwoven with the LGBTQIA+ community that most punk people I've met aren't cisgender heterosexual, they're some colour of the rainbow and are open to the colour that I am too.

So when I see someone dressed in that sort of fashion, I already trust them more, since punks are some of the nicest people I've ever met, even though they're the kind of people that typical adults think are intimidating or dangerous. Crazy how wearing some spikes can be a symbol of acceptance, isn't it? The ones in the mohawks and leather will be the first ones to say, 'I'm adopting you, I'm your new parent,' to young punks like me, who have been cast out by the environments they were raised in. I know from first-hand experience that being 'adopted' by established punks can mean the world when you have no one else to give you that kind of support. It really feels like finding family. Punk is a community of misfits helping misfits, minorities standing together and fighting for acceptance and equality. Every time I step into a crowd that already has its mosh pit in full swing, I feel euphoric, as though I'm surrounded by members of my real family rather than my bigoted biological one.

To me, gender euphoria is the feeling I get when I look in the mirror and think, *Oh yeah, that is me.* Gender euphoria is when I don't keep count of how many feminine or masculine items I'm wearing; I just wear what I want and don't care what others think. Gender euphoria is being called by my preferred name and pronouns and knowing that I'm actually seen as genderless. It's making earrings out of oestrogen or testosterone bottles and showing off top-surgery marks like battle scars. It's Laura Jane Grace burning her birth certificate on stage; it's Billie Joe Armstrong singing about cross-dressing and coming out; it's audiences throwing rainbow and trans flags onto stages and performers displaying them proudly. Euphoria is the rush I get every time I add a patch to my jacket, every time I messily put on eyeliner, every single time I show some skin and feel sexy doing so. Euphoria is when I look in the mirror and I don't see a girl or a boy, I just see me smiling back.

Playing Roller Derby on an All-Girls Team

Laura Kate Dale

Growing up, in the decades prior to my transition, I never really understood the appeal of team sports. I would play football or rugby in school sports lessons when forced to do so, but would equally look for ways to get out of having to take part whenever possible. Faked illnesses, deliberately forgetting sports kits, 'mistakenly' getting my class times mixed up, or turning up to lessons but not engaging with the games being played were all too common parts of my childhood.

Mandatory school team sports basically signified everything I struggled to connect with as an in-the-closet trans girl with coordination issues and, at the time, undiagnosed autism: macho lad culture, bitter competitiveness, the need to be precise with your body moves, getting muddy, getting changed around men, and a need to communicate well in loud, chaotic, crowded settings. The boys I was paired up with were all excited for what was to come, and I couldn't help being aware of how much I didn't feel at ease.

For the longest time I assumed I inherently disliked sports. I came to associate team sports with being reminded how much I wasn't like the men I was paired up with, how much I disliked my body being visible, how much I struggled with the sensory aspects of outdoor sports on grass, and how much I struggled to feel at home with teams I was made a part of.

That is, until I discovered roller derby.

For those unaware of roller derby, it's a team sport, played on roller skates on an indoor circular track. Picture the contact level of rugby but played at high speed, on wheels. One player on each team is the 'jammer', whose job is to do laps of the other team to score points, and the rest of each team is focused on keeping the other team's jammer from getting past, and making openings for their team's jammer. There's a lot of fast skating, dodging and bashing into each other forcefully. It's fast, it's pretty unforgiving, and it's all about teamwork.

Roller derby is a sport played worldwide, mostly by women, and is an overwhelmingly LGBTQIA+ friendly sport. A lot of the women who play the sport are not straight, a lot of leagues around the world have explicit policies protecting the rights of trans and non-binary skaters to play competitively, and those playing the sport are eager to make sure that reputation is earned.

I got into playing roller derby quite by accident a few years ago. I had been out as trans for several years, I had friends, but I didn't really have any hobbies outside of my job. I wanted something I could do a couple of times per week for fun, but I never thought that something would be sports.

I went along to my first roller-derby session more out of support for another trans woman than any actual thought I might stick with the sport long term. This friend of mine had gone to one session and was feeling nervous about going back, so I offered to come along with her and try a session out too. She never actually went back to playing roller derby, but from that first practice session on borrowed gear, I was hooked.

The all-female roller derby team I joined were instantly very accepting of me as a skater, despite my visibly trans status, and the fact I barely had enough balance to get from the edge of the hall into the centre without falling flat on my ass. From helping me up when I fell to cheering me on for making basic minor improvements, they straight away made me feel like failure was an acceptable part of the road to success. I didn't have to worry I would be shouted at for not being good enough yet, and I was going to get support for trying, and improving little by little. This was exactly the kind of supportive female energy I needed to start enjoying team sports.

Very shortly after I joined, pride month rolled around, and practically my whole team were out in full force, flags flying high. Watching my fellow skaters zoom around our home town with pride flags waving, not batting an eye at my trans pride flag, helped me feel reassured I was going to be welcome here.

I had a lot of anxiety about joining an all-female sports team before starting to play roller derby, which I think is understandable. Whenever trans people and sports are mentioned in the same breath on social media or in news coverage, it's usually in an attempt to discredit both our gender and the legitimacy of any victories we may be lucky enough to enjoy. A lot of people will say they're open to transgender people taking part in gendered sports, but as soon as one trans person wins a single sporting event, the whole narrative flips.

Transgender people have an unfair advantage in sports. If we're going to let trans people play in gendered leagues, no cisgender athlete will ever get to win an award ever again. They should be relegated to their own league for trans athletes. They shouldn't play with us.

The moment trans people do well at sport, their victories are usually waved away as either being a result of hormones they had before transition, or hormones they now take after transition. You can play, but if you ever win an event you can expect to be vilified for it.

When initially playing roller derby in the UK, I actually spoke to one of my instructors about this concern, and she was very eager to reassure me this wasn't something I should worry too much about. No matter how good I got at the sport, the league I played in would have my back.

In the UK, I skate as part of the WFTDA, the Women's Flat Track Derby Association, which has on more than one occasion, in response to transphobic news stories regarding sport, put out statements defending the right of trans and non-binary skaters to skate, and thrive, in their league.

As wonderful and affirming as it was to be able to be part of a team of women playing sports together, the biggest moment of gender euphoria I experienced in my time playing roller derby was when I got designated a 'sister'.

So, for a little bit of background information, when you first start playing roller derby in the UK, you have to go through several months of training, labelled your 'fresh meat' period. Over several weekly sessions you have to tick off a bunch of skills to show you are able to do the basic techniques needed in main practices with the team, as well as demonstrating you can skate safely and consistently when the sport ramps up to contact practice.

It all starts off pretty basic, tasking skaters with skating around the track clockwise and anticlockwise, stopping on command without falling, making quick turns, crouching, stepping sideways, and being hit from the side while staying on your feet. By the end of your training you're being tested on things like your endurance skating at speed for long periods of time. There's one test in particular, your 'twenty-seven in five', in which you have to skate twenty-seven laps of the track in five minutes, showing your fitness has reached a threshold to keep up with the rest of the players on your squad.

Now, when you finish up your fresh-meat training and move up to skating with the main team, the change can initially be a bit daunting. Everyone's skating faster and more confidently than you, warm-up routines are more physically draining, contact drills are more intense, and you'll be expected to practise more high-level techniques you might not previously have had to use. There's a lot to learn, and a lot you're expected to pick up fast.

The solution? The big sister/little sister system.

The idea is pretty simple: a newly graduated fresh-meat skater is paired with a more experienced skater who has been a part of the squad for a long time, who is prepared to keep an eye on the newbie and make sure they're keeping up. They can answer questions, give tips, make sure everything makes sense, and offer to be a practice partner for two-skater drills. It's a mentoring system, but it's also a way to help someone new break into an established group of friends who already know each other well. It helps make the team less of a clique, with new skaters integrating with established skaters.

Now, it might seem silly, but I got a huge amount of gender euphoria when I moved up to the main skating team, largely as a result of the naming system used for mentoring. I have siblings, but I grew up with them seeing me as their brother. I know my siblings now refer to me as their sister, but I never really got a chance to develop a bond with them as sisters in the way you do when living together. Roller derby provided a space for me to explore that sisterly bond.

Every week at practice, I would show up in the changing room and my big sister would welcome me over to sit by her. We would kit up while talking about our weeks, how life was going, have a big hug, and get out on the court together to get warmed up.

As simple as it is, having a shared interest and a supportive, friendly bond with another woman, one where we referred to each other regularly as sisters, was a really magical thing. It helped cement the feeling of sisterhood I eventually developed with the wider team as a whole. By giving everyone interwoven sister connections to each other, we all had someone to look out for us, and someone to look out for. It was feminine family, and that was something affirming to make a part of my life.

While roller derby as a sport is fairly aggressive and full on, that sisterly supportive energy very much permeates through my time playing the sport. Between rounds, when we're sitting on the bench regrouping, we all assess who's ready to get back out and who needs to rest with pep talks, strategy discussion, and breaking down what went right and wrong during the last jam. When out on the track, you and your teammates have to very literally support each other, forming strong, agile walls that the other team won't break through. You need to be able to trust your sisters to know instinctively what you're planning and help you achieve it. It's a sport you can't get good at through solo practice alone. No matter which of your sisters you're paired up with, you need to know you can trust them, and offer support tailored to their style of play.

Playing men's team sports, there's an idea of brotherhood between teammates. In roller derby, I found a love for a team sport thanks to being welcomed into a sisterhood. It may not seem so different, but it made a world of difference to me.

Fashion, Gender and Not Knowing You're Non-Binary in Nigeria

Olu Niyi-Awosusi

Twenty-eight, software developer, writer, philomath, Londoner

Oppressive heat, the relief of air conditioning, and a heavy sadness. The punctuation of my time in Nigeria. Not the sadness I should have been feeling, sure, but it was something. My grandma on my mother's side, a woman I barely knew but who I had heard much about, had died a month before.

We were in Nigeria for a funeral I never ended up going to. Some mix-up with the seamstress left me and my sister without outfits to wear. We spent most of the funeral inside the car, on the off-chance the clothes would be sent to us in time.

Nigerian traditional clothing is gendered, though not in fabric or colour choices. For the funeral we were all supposed to wear the same fabric, a pearlescent blue. The styles were chosen by my mother after our measurements had been taken. I never enjoyed the pomp and circumstance of having clothing fitted in my mid-teens. This was no exception. I had little input in what I was supposed to wear, mostly through lack of interest.

For me, then, clothes were a means to an end. They weren't a vehicle for expressing myself. They were a way of doing the least possible to cover my body, and not much else. This was partially due to not feeling I had the capacity to look how I wanted, due to many factors. Lack of money, my body, my race, all tessellated together into a feeling that clothes would never look good on me in the way they did on others.

I think my gender feelings contributed to this; I just wanted to be seen as the same as my close female friends, and so I put on a gender that didn't always sit right with me. Eventually those same girls dragged me into shops and dressed me up, and gave me the first glimmers of insight into how I could conjure the feeling of euphoria with a few well-chosen items of clothing and accessories whenever I liked.

Though I would have referred to myself as a girl or young woman if asked at the time, I never had a strong attachment to any particular gender in private. I existed as a negation – 'not a boy' – rather than by positive affirmation. It took me years to come to the point where I could put words to the feeling. In university, a housemate asked me what I preferred to be called – Girl? Woman? Guy? Man? – as a joke. I replied 'person', and seriously started considering I might not be cis after that point, having just been introduced to other genders as a possibility.

My mother has never directly said anything about my gender. She doesn't know I'm agender or non-binary, and I don't think she'd have anything good to say about it. The only member of my family who knows anything about this side of me is my sister, and even she is not the most understanding when it comes to gender issues.

My mother and I would just clash over the markers of gender that I could manipulate easily. My hair, for example, she wanted me to grow as long as possible and keep straight. I wanted to experiment. It became a minor battleground. First I cut the long, straight, relaxed length into a bob, then at university I cut off the straight hair entirely and let my hair return to its curly state.

Clothes were also a point of tension between my mother and me. She would prefer I made myself look 'pretty'. She wanted me to do many things in this vein, things that took more effort than they were worth, in my view. She tried to cajole me into wearing bright colours and interesting shapes. I was much more comfortable in my customary 'black, or whatever fits' uniform.

During my time in Nigeria the heat was the top dictator of what we wore. Next came what was on sale in the department stores we visited when we did the huge shop before leaving the UK. Lastly, what would fit in the family's communal suitcases. I remember agreeing to many purchases, so many they blurred. I remember folding things into neat, small piles. I remember my brother asking if we'd have to bring forks. I didn't really believe

I'd shortly be touching down in a place as foreign to me as it was familiar to my mother.

My mother had done her best to raise us as Nigerians who only happened to live in England; we ate a lot of Nigerian food, went to church at least once a week, and watched African Entertainment Television and other Nigerian-adjacent channels whenever my mother or stepfather got control of the television. She had a food shop that sold African and Caribbean food when I was a kid, so I was surrounded by honorary aunts and uncles at all times, speaking in Yoruba, the language my mother's people spoke in Nigeria. I never learned Yoruba. I learned to fear and love God and my parents, but was left with confused feelings about how a loving God could think what the pastor was preaching about gay and otherwise queer people.

I was born and raised in the UK, in Luton, only leaving for a handful of school trips within the UK, and one as far as France and Belgium. I relished these trips away from home, always resigned to the inevitable moment I'd have to return to normality.

The trip to Nigeria is decidedly neutral in my memory in comparison. The plane ride over was long, as I couldn't sleep on our red-eye flight. I remember being cold, dressed as I was for the heat of Nigeria and not the controlled temperature of the cabin.

Walking out of the plane into Nigeria itself was a bizarre experience. The heat and humidity of the air was like night and day compared to the dry, cool evenness of the cabin. It must have been even stranger for my mother.

She hadn't been able to visit for visa reasons for my whole life. I was fifteen years old at the time. How did it feel for her to be back for the first time under such terrible circumstances? Her grief was cloying, hard to comprehend, all-encompassing. Above all, from the outside it seemed numb. I don't remember many tears, but I remember a coldness I had rarely felt from her before.

There were glimmers of good in the grief, though. Climbing Olumo Rock. Hearing the story of how, a generation or two ago, Nigerians had hidden under it during bombing in the Second World War. Drinking too-sweet soft drinks. Contrasting them with the Nigerian Fanta we knew and loved. Eating anything and everything. Wondering at how bad some of the Western-style food was. The beautiful landscapes. The crash of storm-ravaged waves on a sandy beach. Meeting cousins we hadn't seen in a few years who had moved there.

We visited many family members. Lots of honorary ones who were more friends of my mother's and stepfather's than anything else. A gaggle of blood aunts, who were thrilled to meet me. They often did not speak much English, sometimes by choice. Even when they did, conversation was brief and filled with smiles.

One of these visits took us to Victoria Island, in the city of Lagos, Nigeria's capital. It was a change from the compounds of my family members. The horrific traffic did little to trample my mood that day. Victoria Island felt more familiar than anywhere else I had visited.

We were there to visit a technical aunt and a technical uncle. They lived in a flat with a communal pool – not as big as the one at a hotel we'd stayed at, but staffed and clean and inviting. I was impressed. Compound living, where everyone lived behind walls and in their own separate patch of land, didn't suit me. We went everywhere with family, unable to even take a walk around the block, as we'd have to be driven. Visiting my aunt and uncle was no exception.

On arriving at the flat, my aunt took one long look at my outfit. She said that I'd need to change as my 'uncle wouldn't like it'. While I didn't react to this at the time, I realise now that the only 'offensive' thing about how I was dressed was the deep V-neck of my black floral top. It didn't even cross my mind to complain about having to change at the time. She said it in a friendly enough way, and I hadn't taken it as a slight on my character.

My aunt's flat was so fancy! She invited me into a neat, small bedroom. She offered me a few brand-new tops from the recesses of a mirrored closet. I picked a Lacoste polo shirt, pink and green with a white collar. It wasn't the kind of thing I would usually wear, but I liked it best of the options.

She left me alone to put it on. I squeezed into it. I stopped, looking at myself in the wall of mirrors. I felt like I was walking on air for a second. For some reason, that outfit sparked off the most intense gender euphoria I have felt in my life.

I had a string of coral paper beads around my neck. I was wearing khaki combats. My mum had ironed them after an argument about how they were 'supposed' to look – crumpled, according to me. I'd had long, thin Senegalese twists done in my hair, in anticipation of the funeral. Of course, I had the polo shirt. I'd chosen items of clothing I had liked individually in the past, sure, but this was the first time the whole of an outfit, and the whole of myself, felt cohesive.

It made my reflection finally click with what I felt inside for the first time. I finally understood that clothing could make me feel better, more whole, more alive. The look was a lot butcher than what I would have guessed would make me feel good about myself at the time. I thought I wanted to emulate the looks of my stylish friends, to be the height of effortless, European girlhood. What makes me feel euphoria now, I guess, is the almost-androgyny that I had for a while that day. What I've always been reaching for. It has proven elusive.

Fashion hadn't been important to me before that point. It became more and more so as I got older and knew myself better. 'Hard femme', 'comfort femme' and other associated labels opened a world of glitter, fancy-yet-comfortable trainers, mesh and sequins. If I couldn't look how I dreamed of looking, I could weave a world where my body fitted my presentation, and claw out a comfortable space for my whole self to fit.

Clothing in general has always been difficult to reconcile with my gender identity. My large chest means I've always felt intensely gendered in most clothing. I've never experimented with binding or considered top surgery. This has led to a feeling of being stuck. I like my chest as an artefact of my body, but not always as a feature to be highlighted in clothing.

I wouldn't have thought it was a gender feeling per se at the time. I hadn't yet read Milan Kundera's book *The Unbearable Lightness of Being*, but years later a line would ring true. It was about a character looking in the mirror and seeing herself as she wished to: 'Each time she succeeded was a time of intoxication: her soul would rise to the surface of her body like a crew charging up from the bowels of a ship, spreading out over the deck, waving at the sky and singing in jubilation.'

In that moment, I was exactly where and who I was supposed to be. I looked 'correct', felt correct, and for once in my life I believed it was a feeling that was accessible to me. At least in theory. This experience sowed the seeds of gender exploration that I would unpack years later.

The Myth of the Yak: Learning to Love My Body Hair

Yas Lime

A hairy, brown, autistic, agender person,
who works as an artist-curator

Being hairy creates and leads the way for my euphoria. My leg hair reminds me of wildflower meadows. My head hair is long pond grass. My armpit hair is a hawthorn bush. My pubic hair is wet moss and lichen on a rock. I sit on a sofa in a restaurant and see people staring. I enjoy it when my gender identity confuses people; I think it's important to push people's perceptions of gender.

As a brown non-binary person I have had to understand that growing my hair naturally allows me to be happy in myself. Not only this, but thinking about hair allows me to be imaginative – to draw, write and photograph myself in a way that shows my true self. This is what makes me truly euphoric.

My birth name is Yasmyn, and any time we were learning the letters of the alphabet, Y would be represented by the humble yak. They're hairy, but they're still beautiful. That always stuck with me. As I grow older I feel more of an affinity with yaks.

My head wasn't shaved when I was born. Muslim parents usually shave the hair of a newborn baby. They weigh the amount shaved and convert it into gold for charity. This did not happen to me – my locks were spared. As I have grown, I have realised how important hair is for every religion, not just for Muslims like my family. Muslims see hair as the most beautiful (and sexual) part of a person, and so to cover it when you come of age promotes a pious life. People of many religions around the world focus on their hair as a symbol of modesty and ritual. Some Jewish women shave their hair when they marry; many Sikhs cover their hair with a turban and do not get rid of any hair at all; Jain monks pluck each hair out of their heads; Catholic nuns cover their hair with habits – the list goes on. Growing up, I looked around at the people in my life, those who chose to cover their hair, and those who did not. I've realised that the most contested area is a woman's head and the strands of keratin that grow out of it. I now have the privilege of knowing that I can do whatever I wish with my hair. But it has been a journey to get here.

I was an avid reader as a child, hoovering up any books I could get my hands on.

I snuck a copy of *The Vagina Monologues* from a bookcase when I was around fourteen. I remember the story of a woman who was asked to shave her pubic hair by her boyfriend; apparently that was the only way that he could get turned on. I remember the writer commenting that it was strange how he would admit this – being attracted to an unshaved vulva. I agreed. I liked the sign of adultness that hair was. Even though it was very uncomfortable for her – itchy, red, raw – she continued to shave herself, as she wanted to be with and please her boyfriend. As an intimate, first-person tale I thought that this was an unusual occurrence – seemingly worthy of its own story. But now that I am older, I realise that the exact opposite is true. These kinds of stories are far from rare.

Reading such a frank tale made me feel euphoric, knowing that these issues were allowed to be discussed – and that there was not only one right way for a person to relate to their body hair.

Even so, every partner I've had has asked me about my body hair, seemingly uncomfortable with the idea of being with a partner who is hairier than them.

'Aren't you getting rid of it?'

'We are going to a wedding – will you have your hairy legs out?'

'Your moustache is showing.'

'You should cover up.'

Many times I would give in to these requests, as I felt I had no choice. I wanted to be loved, and this sometimes meant sacrificing my happiness and my sense of self.

Sometimes that's life? Right?

But the times when I refused, claiming, 'Well, I like it

that way!' or simply stating, 'It's staying,' were the times I felt most in control, and euphoric.

I recently moved house, and I'm currently sharing my home with a guy roughly my own age. I spoke to him while writing this essay, about the fact I was going to be writing about my relationship with my body hair, and he said to me that when he dated a girl, he felt the need to keep his legs hairy, even though he preferred to shave his legs. He prefers the feeling of a smooth leg for himself. Now he is single, he shaves his legs. Similarly, my uncles from hot countries shave their legs regularly, as they see it as more hygienic when sweating in the summer sun.

However, every time I looked at other people and their relationship to their body hair, the question I asked myself was, *Why don't I get to choose?* The choice that guys make about their hair usually doesn't get questioned, or at least they have more options open to them. It was refreshing to hear that even cis straight guys sometimes feel a struggle with the rigid expectations of their gender.

My choice, on the other hand, to keep my hair was constantly questioned. I was lazy or unclean – something was wrong with me because I didn't want to shave.

The illusion of gender was a mirage for me from a young age. Glitches in the system like this, gendered expectations and double standards, proved to me that gender was not prescriptive, and that these double standards could be questioned. Importantly, the boundaries of what was acceptable could be pushed. I never saw it as a crusade or something that I was doing to change the world. Keeping my hair natural was something I did for myself, and it just felt right.

I first became aware of my level of body hair when I went to summer camp. We went to a swimming pool with young people from around the world. I remember the thin, white girls – seemingly hairless. And looking down at my legs, I noticed the hair that I had inherited was thick, black and coarse. Like Adam and Eve expelled from the Garden of Eden, I felt shame in myself, an embarrassment that I had rarely felt.

I did not realise how significant that difference was until I was old enough to notice the models in advertisements for razors and deodorants. They were hairless and had no shave marks, no stubble either, nor the occasional single long chin hair like I got. I would always think to myself, *How did they get it like that?* Whiteness was the default, and naturally, white people have less-visible body hair – so I thought that it was the norm. I saw adverts for razors and bizarrely, they would be shaving an already smooth leg!

So was I not normal, then? In my time I've taken razors, scissors, epilators, hot and cold wax, tweezers and bleaching cream to my skin in order to try and look more like those white female models. I was told it was cleaner, and ultimately more womanly, to do so. No man would ever want to be with a hairy person. Being hairy was tantamount to being unkempt and unclean. All I remember is the itchiness! The razor cuts! The cream burns! The pain!

For an autisic person, these things were like torture. My sensory alarms were triggered every single time I tried to achieve those stubble-lacking legs. My hair was so thick, any attempt to remove it would mean an hour's work, easily. The razors would blunt after a few strokes!

This, mixed with a heady bout of gender dysphoria caused by trying to be a 'woman', meant body hair became my own personal battleground.

What is interesting to me as I get older is the double standards parents and guardians set for the children in their care. For example, 'Don't give into peer pressure,' and, 'Be yourself.' Both important life lessons we are taught, yet the moulds and expectations we put on to a child's AGAB (assigned gender at birth) is one big mess of expectations and pressures. I hope any children I eventually help raise (hello – if you're reading this) will know that they can call me out on double standards and be themselves, growing their hair as they wish and expressing themselves in a way that feels right for them.

I rebelled as a child against heteronormativity, religion, the patriarchy – any type of authority, in fact. As I grew, I started posing questions about hair to the women in my family. I started looking at the boys around me. Were they dirty? Unkempt? Unclean? Their hair was worn as a badge of pride. When they stretched their arms up in summer, thick clumps sprouted from their pits. I didn't consciously know it at the time, but I envied them. They celebrated their first chest hair, their first curly pubic hair – no matter how small – whereas I was told this was a shameful and disgusting part of myself to be culled. I longed for the freedom to be able to leave it as it was, to be myself. The problem was I didn't even know that was an option.

Now I know that if that is my wish, it can be granted by none other than my own fairy godparent – myself!

There was a time where I lived in Brighton, UK, a very queer-friendly and eccentric city on the south coast. A phrase I often used while living there was 'you will never be the most eccentric one in Brighton'. Whatever I wore, I was always outdone. I think this is what gave me the confidence I needed to start to wear outfits that showed off my legs as I let my body hair grow out. It was freedom, a space to discover how free and confident I felt, letting my body exist the way it was born to. No one was looking at my legs. The spotlight was never on me. I was free to simply be.

I'd been battling for years with my relationship to my own body hair, but during those years of exploring my outward presentation I could feel that there was something else bubbling in the undercurrents. Surprise! It was my gender identity – and specifically my lack of one. When I started seeing the term 'non-binary' and learning about non-Western, indigenous forms of gender – such as two-spirit[*] – it clicked. Agender, non-binary, it is what I am

[*] A term rooted in spiritual beliefs used by some Native Americans to describe a person who doesn't fit the gender binary.

– and what I have always been. I now wear skirts and shorts whenever it's warm enough, with my legs proudly displayed, hairy as they may be. The freedom that I saw in the youth of boys, I am now able to feel. To me, I hope my hair signifies to the world that I am not restricted to the feminine ideal of Western beauty. I hope it confuses people and perhaps lets people of all ages know that they also do not need to feel restricted or confined into one gendered space.

When I asked, at the place where I used to get my eyebrows waxed, 'Could I get my moustache done too?' the person who was doing the treatment hastily said to me, 'You mean your upper lip?' I thought to myself that I didn't realise that this part of our body was gendered. To me, hair is just hair – when is a moustache not a moustache? Hair grows out of all of our skin. Hair is gendered. But as an agender person, I have always had difficulties with that. And it's only now, after twenty-five years, that I am completely at ease and in love with my hair.

I now am starting to see artists depicting people as their full hairy selves. This is what I aspire to do – using hair in my own mixed-media practice. I enjoy using actual strands of my own hair encased in wax and glue. The glue strands and the hair mimic the shapes and curves of each other. I also enjoy taking very close-up photographs of the hairs on my chin and my moustache. This practice highlights my hair as a necessary and integral part of myself. Not something to be hidden away or got rid of, but something to be zoomed into, stared at and admired.

Growing to Appreciate Myself in Photographs

Laura Kate Dale

For the first couple of decades of my life, it was pretty tough to get a nice-looking photograph of me. I was an anxious and awkward child, and whenever it was time for me to smile for a camera, I'd put on this big, almost comical exaggerated grin. I didn't know how to make a smile look natural. I performed a smile as best I could.

During the bulk of my childhood, before I came out as trans, I tried to avoid looking at myself as much as possible. Most of the time it wasn't even out of any particular hatred of how I looked – I just didn't really connect with the image I saw reflected back at me. It didn't matter if my outfit clashed, or if my hair was neatly brushed, or if my smile looked awkward. Those were things other people expected of my appearance. I didn't really have much connection to my own appearance.

When you have a body that you feel awkward inhabiting, and that awkwardness labels you as different from the people around you who you most easily emotionally connect with, your body becomes something you just try to pretend doesn't exist. At least, that was the case for me.

It's hard to care about how you look when you don't feel a connection to your own body. Without that sense of ownership, my physical appearance was often an afterthought, and the idea of preserving snapshots of that appearance wasn't really something I considered important.

I loved taking photographs as a child and a teenager, but they were never centred on myself or my friends. I would take wildlife stills; I would photograph objects and events. I would use photos to remember nice days, or places I might not revisit. But I wouldn't photograph people so much. I'd never liked seeing myself in pictures, and it was hard to imagine other people liking themselves in pictures either. I just didn't quite make the mental connection that my dislike of appearing in photographs might not be a normal trait.

The first time I ever remember actively wanting to be photographed it was less because of my appearance and more as a way to remember something I had worked hard on making. I got into cosplay – the art of making costumes based on anime or video-game characters, generally to be worn at conventions – in my late teens. As a shy kid who wasn't quite out as trans yet, cosplay offered a social safety-net topic for making friends, and a creative outlet that I could pour myself into. I spent countless hours cutting and stitching together fabric, scouting out cheap props, designing replica items and putting together all the pieces of elaborate costumes, and it was one of the first non-academic pursuits I really found fulfilling to put my time into.

I remember, a couple of years into cosplaying for conventions, my mother pointing out that despite how many costumes I was making and wearing to events, there were rarely nice pictures of me at those events for her to look at. So I let her do a photo shoot of me and a friend in our costumes before heading to an event. I had the safety net of a character and outfit to hide behind. I could copy poses that characters used in the show. I had an image to emulate when trying to take a nice photograph. In one of my costumes I had a full face-covering helmet on, which meant I didn't even have to worry about my awkward smile.

As it turns out, when I wasn't looking like myself I actually quite enjoyed being in photographs. When the character in the photographs wasn't an awkward, uncomfortable, pre-transition teenager, I quite liked the idea of taking the time to capture my appearance. I wasn't nearly as opposed to being in photographs as I had always assumed.

A couple of years later, when I eventually started to come out as trans to my friends and family, photographs acted as a lifeline, something to keep my sense of validity as a woman intact during a spell of my life where being out full time as female wasn't really an option.

When I first came out as trans I was living at home with my parents still. I was not a well-behaved child at the time, and I caused a lot of issues for my parents. My living full time as Laura at home was contingent on me reaching certain milestones within my home life, plus there was a period where I was out to my friends but not yet to my family. The end result: there were multiple years in my early transition where my life as female was compartmentalised. I was Laura at certain times, and at other times had to put that part of myself away and be someone else.

As someone who had hated being in photographs for a lot of my life, this is where I came to first really understand their importance, and the importance of a good selfie.

Early on in transition, I used to attend a local trans support group that happened across town from me on a pretty regular basis. It was a space for trans people of varying ages, and at differing points in their journeys as trans people, to come together and talk about things that they were struggling with, support each other, and make each other feel better about themselves.

One night in particular with the group that really stood out to me was a pyjama party organised by a few of the group. Everyone could show up in nice comfy PJs, and there were a variety of activities organised to offer little gender-affirming moments to those attending. We could have our hair, nails and make-up done by professionals without having to pay, and could then, at the end of the night, have a photograph taken, which would be printed and collected later.

I still have that photograph printed out, sitting in a drawer in my office. Looking back at it, my make-up was a bit excessive and not really in keeping with the sense of fashion and style I eventually developed, but what it represented at the time was hope and promise. It was a photograph where I had taken that same care and attention over my appearance as I had in those old cosplay pictures, but without trying to play a character. The person in the photo was me. I loved taking time that night to think about how I looked, and I loved getting to feel that I looked nice. I loved that it gave me hope that one day, this could be how I looked every day.

In that photograph, I have the biggest, most natural smile. It's probably the only photo from that time where my smile looks that genuine. I had found a pocket of happiness and I had a reminder of it.

For the years that followed, until I was able to start living full time as Laura, that photograph went everywhere with me, tucked inside a DVD case to keep it from getting damaged, in the bottom of my bag. Any time I needed a reminder, something to tell myself that the woman I was existed and would one day get to shine, I would sneak a quick look. I took a few more photos in those early years, when I found particularly cute and gender-affirming outfits to wear, but that first photograph was the one that always felt most important to me.

When I eventually started living as an out trans woman fully, I initially went a little wild with taking selfies. Everything I could do with my appearance was new and exciting, and selfies became a really nice way for me to document looks that worked for me, and to narrow down what my sense of style was. I learned that jackets over colourful tops looked really nice on me. I discovered that I looked better photographed from slightly above. I realised that it was a lot easier to smile if I actually liked what I saw when looking at my reflection.

Where I had first learned to love being photographed as a result of cosplaying, I found that those cosplay weekends continued to be a really great space to learn to love my appearance. I could wear multiple different gender-affirming outfits in the space of a single weekend, around friends who could help bring out the best of my appearance, and would always be there to make me feel great about the way I looked along the way. I was in a setting where everyone looked excessive and over the top, so I could play around with feminine looks that I would be nervous to try day to day. With everyone in silly outfits, I had a playground to explore what I might look like with a pixie cut, or neon hair, or in shorter skirts, or holding a fake replica sword. For the record, I can really rock the 'sword-wielding biker lesbian' look, apparently – thanks, anime conventions for teaching me that one.

These days I have settled into a fashion sense I am comfortable with and I frequently have days where I love how I look. I have favourite selfies, and favourite outfits, and there are days where I just revel in how awesome I have come to look over the years since I transitioned.

Today, rather than an awkward teenager wearing all black and trying not to be noticed, I wear big stompy biker boots that make me even taller than my six-foot height. I wear black denim jackets over bright colourful shirts. I recently shaved one side of my head really short, and I now rock asymmetrical, bright blue hair that years ago I would never have had the confidence to consider. Sometimes I instead wear big, flowing, comfortable, neon, hippy comfort clothes. No matter my style, I dress to be seen. I dress to no longer be invisible.

I wear the outfits I do today because I love seeing myself in a reflection in a window as I pass a car. I dress for the glimpses of myself, and the smile they bring to my face. I dress the way I do because I love getting to take a snapshot of the me I am today, confident and badass and loving her life. Where the photos of me prior to transition often look like I'm being held hostage in the frame, there out of necessity rather than joy, I look at photos of myself as an adult, and see a woman who's in the frame for herself, not for anyone else.

That's someone I want to take photos of. I want to photograph a woman who's excited to be seen. I want to see the smile of a version of myself who is ecstatic every day to be who she is.

The Gates to Jannah: Balancing Transitioning and My Faith

Jaden Hameed

Twenty-four, disabled trans man living in Colombo, Sri Lanka

As a Muslim, the word Jannah has been a recurring theme in my life. Entering Jannah, or heaven, is often what believers strive for during their temporary life on earth. There is a list of things Muslims can do that will jeopardise our chances of entering heaven, aside from being unapologetically evil – which, by default, will earn you a place in hell.

I was not the 'good' child my Sri Lankan Muslim family hoped for. I was certainly not the good *girl* my family wanted me to be. Though I didn't know it at the time, I was very much trans. The only reason why I didn't realise it sooner was because I was always treated like an average cis boy due to my mischievous behaviour during most of my childhood.

While this kind of behaviour wasn't a problem initially, my mischief eventually got to a point where everyone would chide me with some iteration of this: 'Behave yourself! If you don't, you will never reach the gates of Jannah!' At the time, I didn't really know what this would entail.

I wasn't particularly religious growing up, but whenever I had a problem I couldn't solve, I would turn to God. Most Muslims follow the methods of *salat* (Islamic prayer) devoutly; not me! I'd put out the *sajjada* (prayer mat) and treat *salat* like a phone call to Allah.

I was very nonchalant with theology, and my unwillingness to follow the rules led to me struggling with my religion at quite a young age. I was an outcast among fellow Muslims. I was too 'modern', too 'casual' with my faith. 'You can't even read Arabic! What are you going to do when the angels open the Qur'an and place it before you?'

They didn't know I was struggling with dancing letters that never stayed still on pages; they didn't know I couldn't visualise an apple in my head, or recognise a 'familiar' face I hadn't seen in a short while. They didn't know that climbing down the stairs was scary because it looked more like a flat plane than actual steps. They'd bully me and repeat that tired old mantra of how I would never enter Jannah. I was a 'sinner' in their eyes. This only pushed me further from religion.

But even then, I didn't abandon Islam... not just yet.

I reached the pinnacle of my struggle with my belief at age nine, when I read Mary Shelley's *Frankenstein*, and questioned God and all his creations. 'If man could, by some miracle, raise life from nothing more than a piece of his own flesh and a concoction of chemicals, lit up by a spark, then perhaps being God isn't all that difficult,' I told myself. I was convinced that every problem had a logical solution, and every miracle had a 'method' behind it.

I worked hard to fix my issues: I formed my own system to learn things, colour-coded my surroundings mentally so that I could navigate better, and even picked up sports to help me with my motor issues. I was convinced I had everything pinned down.

It took a lot for me to learn that I couldn't control everything in my world. That very year, I came home one day to find my parents crying in the hall, surrounded by hefty files and stacks of loose, yellowed paper. In due time, I would find out that we'd gone bankrupt.

The implications of bankruptcy were very comprehensible to me. No more car, house, nice clothes or trips. Everything had to be rationed. Every step we took thereafter had to be calculated. Thus, as the 'family disappointment', their focus was now completely on me: What's this insolent brat going to do with his life?

Oh, I'll tell you what I did: sweet *nothing*. I took it all for granted! I left my exam papers blank, never listened in class, stopped interacting with people, and my 'phone calls' with Allah were growing increasingly infrequent, because, 'Clearly, good things weren't meant to happen to me, so why bother begging for them?'

The pressure had finally broken me.

The highlight of my year was a trip to the planetarium,

during which I was forcefully pulled out of the girls' line and pushed into the boys' line by a random disciplinarian. 'What are you doing?! Causing trouble for no reason, ah? Here, come stand over here. Useless child!'

I was over the moon. I couldn't stop smiling as we marched towards the planetarium. Perhaps it was my penchant for mischief? Since I couldn't be as unruly as I wanted to any more without being noticed, I took great joy in the little bits of chaos that unfurled by themselves.

Had I known this would be the last time in a long time where somebody would correctly 'mistake' me for a boy, I would have cherished it more.

I entered my teens in a thick hoodie and with a fringe that covered half my face. I spoke very little to most people and had severe social anxiety. I didn't have very much to look forward to, and nothing made me truly happy any more. I cried randomly, got angry often, and started to really hate everything about myself for the first time ever. Welcome home, puberty! You're doing excellent, sweetie.

I recall the shift in the type of conversations my friends would have. We went from talking about the most random, nonsensical things (like cartoons, funny animals, etc.) to talking about boys, periods, breasts, sex and so on, as teenagers eventually do.

'Did you know that when you hit puberty, things start to grow?' one classmate said, voice low, tone cautious.

'What do you mean?' another enquired.

'Well, your... chest. It expands!' she replied.

I'd been silent throughout this exchange, but then I interjected with what I thought would be a unanimous thought. 'I'd like my chest to stay flat. I'd hate it if my breasts appeared.'

The looks of shock on their faces told me my calculations had been way off.

'Are you insane? Ha ha!'

'A woman without breasts? Isn't that weird?'

'Ew, dude!'

The conversation then veered into bathing in rivers for some reason, and I went away to sulk in a corner.

Days turned to weeks, and weeks to months. The changes in my body became more noticeable than ever before. My breasts were a size C cup in just a year. My mother refused to buy me any more bras, as if it were my fault they were growing so rapidly. We really couldn't afford to anyway. We could barely afford to have three solid meals.

She'd cook for the week and freeze the rice and curry in boxes. I often skipped lunch and we'd have this food for dinner. My books were second-hand and my uniforms were far too short for me. But I didn't complain because none of these material things mattered to me any more, at least not as much as they used to. The world had gone sepia. My oyster had been thrown into a pot of boiling water, and then cracked open for the feast.

Basketball was the one thing that helped me feel whole. To be out there, running, sweating and roughhousing with friends; it was a sense of freedom I couldn't experience anywhere else. But with my ever-expanding chest and budget bras, I received a bit of unsolicited attention. It got to the point where a few girls from the basketball team cornered me to give me a talking-to. 'It's so ugly how they just bounce when you run. You better get more supportive bras or it looks disgusting.'

I quit basketball.

I started gaining a lot of weight, and with this, every bit of my body that I wanted to hide grew more conspicuous. I hid away as much as I could. I wore three or four layers of clothing every time I went out for anything at all. My parents would laud it as me being 'conservative' and 'respectful' of my body.

They were hopeful that maybe I hadn't given up on religion entirely just yet, but I was getting there.

See, to me, it was just my feeble attempt at trying to hide my pronounced hips.

I didn't know the word for it then, but I now know it was dysphoria.

I wish it had become less complicated, but no. Life gives you lemons, so you take a big bite and spit the seeds out, only for them to sprout and drop ten hefty fruits on your noggin. I had a series of boyfriends in school, mostly just passing letters to each other and occasionally holding hands. Things were great that way! It was like having a bunch of really close friends... until one guy suggested we have sex. I hadn't even kissed anyone yet!

Anyway, the self-destructive side of me thought, *Why*

not? The attempt led to a complete freak-out on my part, and everything crashed and burned.

So, I'm averse to sex! Good to know.

And so I remained an introverted, scared kid who hated everything about myself for the next few years. But in the year 2017, things took an unexpected turn: an internet friend of mine, Amal, came out to me as trans.

Social media, as we all know, can be a toxic wasteland, but it can also be the provider of a silver lining on a very dark day. This person I'd known online for several years had just come out to me. We had a long chat about it, and I took some time away from everything to think about it. Not because I was transphobic – no! The gears in my head were turning rapidly. Pieces of the puzzle were finally falling into place.

A whole new world had just opened up to me. Growing up in a relatively conservative Muslim family in Sri Lanka, having to rely on what basic necessities I could afford, dealing with my invisible disability and being an overall mess, had dampened my chances of exploring who I really was. But hearing this come from a friend – whom I hold dear to this day – hit close to home.

This wasn't some far-away story on TV. This was somebody I knew and loved. Everything was suddenly very real.

The next day I stood in front of the mirror, like in those short films about trans boys you find on YouTube. I pressed my breasts into my chest with my hands, I prodded my hips. I was on the verge of tears. As I knelt before the mirror, as dramatic as that sounds, for the first time I finally understood what was wrong.

But there was a long road of learning and unlearning ahead, and I was nowhere close to self-acceptance. I'd been taught very different things in madrasa. 'Same-sex relationships are *haram* (forbidden)! A man dressing up as a woman is *haram*! Pre-marital sex is *haram*! Alcohol is *haram*!'

The list of *haram* things I'd done up to this point was already extensive. I made one final phone call.

'Are the gates of Jannah closed for me? When I take this step, if I were to be kinder, more altruistic, more forgiving, will you let me in?' No answer.

Regardless, my mind began to clear up. I felt pure, distilled excitement at the possibilities the future held. Over the next couple of weeks I hinted at my transness to my parents. I gently forwarded articles about trans people and made them watch movies with trans characters. Not a hint of realisation appeared.

Not long after, when I was walking towards my office with my father (this was my first actual job, and I was terrified of going anywhere alone), he saw a trans woman walking alongside us. 'Oh! It's a tr*nny!' he said, tugging at my sleeve to get my attention. A sort of bubbling rage built up inside me, and I snapped in a way I had never done before. I yelled at him, bringing up all the things I wanted to call him out for in one go. This was when I decided to face my fears and move out.

I turned to my friend Amal, who put me in touch with a friend of theirs from Twitter, Corby. Corby was looking for a housemate, and upon hearing about my predicament, instantly agreed to rent out the other room to me.

This move would turn out to be the best decision I would ever make, for multiple reasons. Being around like-minded people helped me get rid of any doubts I'd had about my transness. I learned to accept myself and also bolstered my knowledge about being trans in a safe space where I could ask questions and not feel like I was unwelcome.

We called the house 'Haven', because it was a safe space for anyone who didn't fit the norm. Disabled folk, queer folk, neurodivergent folk, everyone! Here, I could be me. No misgendering, no dead-naming. I could wear what I wanted; I could do what I wanted. Most importantly, for the first time in over ten years, I started to feel content.

Of course, the journey didn't stop there. Socially transitioning was difficult, especially because I wasn't on testosterone yet and didn't really, for lack of a better term, 'pass'. But that step was the first of many tough steps, and it only made me stronger! I persisted.

A year later, my housemate came out as non-binary and married their long-time partner, Amey. They moved in together, which broke up our living arrangement, but following a short, unhappy spell in my parental home, they invited me to stay with them again, and so I moved right back in.

Unhindered by societal expectations, I threw my hands in the air and swaggered around the city, living it up. Not a privilege many of us have, but I was lucky because I had a great support network that enabled this. I went on to meet a bunch of closeted trans people from all walks of life through them, and I'm glad to say I was able to have a positive impact on my trans siblings by being comfortable with myself.

It was beautiful watching other kids like me realise that they could break out of that shell and be embraced for being their most authentic self; to see the sadness lift from their eyes and to witness true joy in them. It's a metamorphosis from which we emerge iridescent.

After much deliberation and research, I was able to begin medically transitioning. It was nerve-wracking, putting myself out there (outside of a queer space), but Amey and Corby helped me through this anxiety.

They facilitated the hospital visit, accompanied me there, sat with me through the appointment, and then we shared a teary moment after I'd received the green light to register at the HRT clinic. They even started a savings account for my surgery and deposited whatever they could every month.

Their friends, who eventually became my friends, also helped raise money for my surgery. Both Amey and Corby stayed by my side while I was recovering from my top surgery at the hospital, and continue looking out for me to this day. I call them 'Ren' and 'Mom' because they're practically my parents – just more proof that a found family is as good, if not better, than a birth family. And this family helped me stand up from the slow crawl towards self-acceptance I was on, and subsequently helped me run.

I guess I've learned and grown a lot over the years. For starters, I've shed the extra layers of clothing because I'm no longer afraid of my body or ashamed of showing a little extra skin. I'm a little more confident in my abilities and a little less worried about what my family, relatives and others around me think of me.

But I also unintentionally learned that the distance that had grown between me and Islam, due to the unforgiving opinions of the less tolerant, could be bridged by a new perspective: queerness and Islam can occupy the same space without cancelling each other out.

Amey, being a queer Muslim herself, led by example. She prays, she recites, she fasts and carries out her Muslim duties, but she never feels the need to apologise for being who she is. She understands that a benevolent God would never shun her for this.

An unexpected positive that came with this new life I'd undertaken was also me learning to not be ashamed of my disability and to learn to work alongside it once again, thanks to the immense support I received from my friends.

Finally, after years of observation, I learned that euphoria can be sourced from a number of little things. It's not just the way I present myself, or my pronouns, or the HRT. It also comes from the way people talk about me.

For example, I enjoyed mischief as a child not because I wanted to be intentionally awful, but because people would always compare me to the other naughty *boys* they knew, and that was affirmation to my young mind. Euphoria is also in the things I do for myself – like playing a sport or singing a song, or writing a story.

In the end, I learned that for me gender euphoria isn't an ocean of good feelings. It's the little waves appearing against the horizon before crashing into nothingness. It shouldn't be mourned, however temporary it is.

Euphoria is a part of the intricate tapestry that is my life, where the good and the bad have to co-exist because that's what makes me, me.

I may have sinned, according to some, by being myself and finally accepting who I am. But then again, I may have sinned by doing a number of other things a Muslim must never do, like hurting a person's feelings or drinking.

Even though it has been a while since I strayed from the *mu'min*'s (believer's) path, and even though my faith may never bounce back to what it used to be, I have to keep trying. As I strive to carve myself a slice of heaven on earth by clawing at any string of happiness I can find, I still hope that if Jannah does exist, its gates will open up for me in the afterlife.

Exploring Gendered Presentation in Online Gaming Worlds

Laura Kate Dale

When I think about the moments of gender euphoria I have experienced in my life, most of them understandably happened during or after the start of my transition. It makes sense: before I came out as trans and started to experiment with female presentation, I was living as male full time, which is not a recipe for a happy and euphoric trans woman.

However, I have one story, from several years prior to my transition, that does have a lot of experiences of gender euphoria tied into it. It was the first domino that fell in a chain of dominos that eventually led to me coming out as trans, and despite a little negativity involved, I largely feel great joy when I think back on this story.

So, let's talk about online video games, and how they provided my first outlet to self-administer moments of gender euphoria.

The year was 2006, and I was around fourteen years old. I was a very shy and insular teenager, and I didn't really have a great grasp on how to socialise with other people in person, but I did know how to socialise in writing. Written communication had clear rules, a lack of ambiguity, and a lot fewer social rules attached to it. I got diagnosed with autism a few years later, which explains a lot of those social struggles, but they were just as much a result of a lack of comfort with who I was day to day. As a result, for a while I got really into playing MMOs.

For the uninitiated, an MMO, or massively multiplayer online game, is a video game played online in a persistent world with other players. You're all usually off doing your own quests and adventures, but you can meet up with your friends, communicate, and work together on big tasks. MMOs are usually as much a social hub as they are a video game. You create your own character, which can either be a representation of yourself or some fantasy alternative, and you play the role of your adventurer in a world shared with others.

I got really into MMOs because they were a space to socialise with friends without having to deal with all the messy in-person stuff. I could google turns of phrase I didn't understand, sarcasm was usually denoted with some highlighted text, and I was able to take time crafting my responses to make sure I didn't say anything that would mess up a conversation. For a few years my MMO of choice was a game called *RuneScape*, mainly because it could be played in a browser and you could get it to run on the computers at school. I played *RuneScape* with my existing school friends – I didn't really make an effort to meet new people in the game – and it basically acted as a stand-in form of socialising.

However, *RuneScape* isn't the MMO that led me to my first experiences of gender euphoria. That experience was thanks to probably the world's best known MMO, *World of Warcraft*.

I originally got into playing *World of Warcraft* because the group of friends I played *RuneScape* with wanted to keep our character levels consistent, meaning I couldn't really sit and play the game for long hours without them. I wanted another game of that type to play, and so I hopped ship to the most popular one I had heard of.

Now, as a fourteen-year-old, I was deeply in denial about being trans. I was in a phase where I went out of my way to present myself as traditionally masculine as best I knew how, to avoid the truth I had spent quite some time dancing around. In real life, I didn't want to acknowledge the fact I wanted to be a woman.

I tried to engage in sports, and learned enough that I could talk about them if asked. I tried to engage more in 'locker-room talk', much to my displeasure. I tried to engage with the scary or gross-out humour movies my male friends wanted to watch. I tried my best to be 'one of the guys', because the alternative was the scary prospect of acknowledging I wasn't.

But, for some reason, booting up *World of Warcraft* on a rain-soaked night, I decided to make a female character to play as.

I can't really explain what brought me to make that

choice. It was definitely in part because I didn't plan to play the game with anyone I knew in real life; I wanted a space to explore my gender presentation without any pressure to come to any firm conclusions or any need to answer questions I wasn't yet ready for. It was probably in part because a *RuneScape* quest around that time had transformed my male player character into a female character, and I had been weirdly disappointed when they ended up getting transformed back. Maybe, and I suspect this was the largest factor, it was just because I was a scared trans girl who knew what she wanted, and no matter how much she tried to deny it, she needed an outlet to explore who she was.

So I created a new character and I jumped in to play. The results were pretty instant. The first time someone in game used female pronouns to refer to me, I felt at home.

By virtue of having picked a feminine-coded screen name, and having a female-presenting character avatar, my interactions with strangers online were very quickly gender-affirming. Online gaming communities are not always great to women, and I had to, on occasion, deal with players telling me I wasn't welcome in their communities, but at the very least other players referred to me as she or her. That was enough for fourteen-year-old me. Something about that felt right. I liked the simple act of being thought of as a woman. It was a lifeline.

Where I had played *RuneScape* with my friends as a fairly insular experience, playing mostly with those I already knew, in *World of Warcraft* I made a much stronger effort to branch out and meet new people. I wanted to build connections and see what friendships felt like on the understanding that I was a woman. I wanted to experience what it was like, being able to share my feelings, my interests and my personality with others without fear that I would be told that wasn't the right way for a boy to behave.

And so life went on for several months. I would stay up as late as I could playing *World of Warcraft*, forging new friendships, get a few hours of sleep, then stumble out of bed to return to school the next morning. I lived two lives for a while, an outward-facing life of deliberate performative hypermasculinity, and a secret online life where I was a woman, and nobody had any reason to think otherwise.

I found myself increasingly frustrated and upset when going back to school, and at the time I couldn't see the very obvious connection which was right in front of my face. The more time I spent online as a woman, the more the performative masculine nonsense became unbearably tiring. I'd glimpsed the other side, and I wanted to reside there. The more I hated my day to day, the more I loved my time online.

I built new friendships, where those I socialised with every night couldn't call me by my birth name, as they had never known it, and had no reason to refer to me with male pronouns. I knew I was safe to just sit with a feeling of comfort for a while. I didn't need to do anything about my feelings, I just loved to sit in the quiet calm that was getting to be seen as a woman. What was euphoric was that the turmoil and confusion I was feeling every day was settling. I had found the calm at the eye of the storm. An oasis in the desert. A place of respite. I was so happy.

World of Warcraft was my first taste of a space where I could present as female safely and regularly, and it was, ultimately, a pretty addictive experience. Looking back, it was pure escapism, a bandage on a much bigger situation. I wanted to be a woman, but I didn't want to accept that I wanted to be a woman; however, I could play a video game, love that experience and write it off as being the video game itself I was enjoying. It was a space to explore who I was, held at arm's reach just enough to plausibly deny.

I didn't stick around playing *World of Warcraft* for too long. The short version of that story is that I had a bit of a falling-out with my online friends in game when they discovered they were playing with someone whose female-coded avatar was a cover for a masculine-coded real-world name. I didn't have the vocabulary at the time to explain that I was a possibly questioning trans woman looking for a space to explore gender presentation. I just sort of apologised, like a kid caught stealing sweets just before dinner, and quietly faded away. It was a shame: I had really enjoyed the avenue for digital escapism, but in the long run I think leaving the game when I did was ultimately for the best. It pushed me to find those moments of euphoria elsewhere, and helped me proceed down the road to coming out as trans.

Without the nudge that I got from playing *World of*

Warcraft as a female character, and feeling joy and calm in being seen as female, I probably wouldn't have had the confidence to try my first few experiences of outwardly presenting as female in the real world, around my friends. Sure, I hid those early experiences under the safety of 'lol, it's just a joke', but those experiences were a direct result of knowing I liked being seen as female.

A couple of years after my experiences with *World of Warcraft*, I decided to dress up as a female character for a costume event, just as a silly joke that definitely shouldn't be taken seriously. A few months after that, I swapped clothes with a friend at school and went with them to an art class, where I spent lunch presenting as female to see if anyone would notice. You know, just as a joke. At that lunch I even used the name Laura for myself. There are Facebook posts I have archived from that time where I joke about how silly it had been. What wasn't silly was the huge smile on my face in the selfie I took that day. It's the happiest-looking photograph of me from that time period by a long shot.

World of Warcraft gave me a safe space to learn that years of wanting to be a woman, when put into practice socially, felt right. It gave me the confidence to see if I felt the same in the real world. *That* gave me the confidence to come out. It was the first gender-euphoria domino on the road to me being the happy and confident woman I am today.

Increasing numbers of video games today allow you to change your character's gender at will, without penalty.

I'm glad to see that, because it really opens up the idea of digital spaces as being safe to explore gender. You can just try a little bit of being gendered a certain way, see if it works for you, no commitment.

I am glad I took a chance and played *World of Warcraft* as a female character. If I hadn't, I don't know if I ever would have known the simple joy of being gendered correctly, and feeling it wash over me like a wave of calm relief. It's where I first found the feeling of being home.

Adrenaline Fix: Turning Masculine Pursuits Into Feminine Identity

Samara-Jade Sendek

She/her, twenty-four, trans woman, from somewhere in Australia

My first memory of gender euphoria was a pastel-pink princess dress in kindergarten. I loved the texture of it, something that tickled my then undiagnosed autism spectrum disorder. Someone decided that it was too girly for me and gave me camouflage tees instead. I didn't pay it no mind. I liked the idea of being a little fighter on a mission. A steady diet of *Dragon Ball Z* and *The Grim Adventures of Billy & Mandy* kept people from guessing I was watching *Winx Club* and *Mew Mew Power* at stupid o'clock in the morning.

Bullies loved my deadname, and they loved that I didn't fit the mould of a small-country-town boy. I didn't kick a football well, and I was bookish and shy. There were plenty of celebrities with feminine versions of my name back then too. I was a bully's choice target at age six, especially without any coping mechanisms. A drunk, ex-reservist father and some antiquated opinions from my mother didn't shield me from society deciding that I wasn't 'manly enough'.

So, my only conclusion was to buy into the same toxic masculinity. 'Drink some concrete and harden the fuck up!' If nobody stood up for me, I'd stand up for myself. I'd be a tough fighter.

Well, the joke was on adult me for buying into that drivel.

Some fifteen years later, in a dull haze of country-town blues and thermonuclear self-hate, gender euphoria cut through the nihilistic shell I'd built for myself. It had been exactly two years since a cardiac episode ended my cage-fighting dreams. I was kicked out of my family home for the second time, now living with my grandma and uncle, who fought weekly. I had thirty minutes to myself every night between work and university, studying game design and production management. After expenses, I had $18 a week to live on. My home area was suffocating me.

I didn't think I could smile any more. My fire – my passions, energy; my life, in a sense – the thing I carried into every training session, had gone out. I didn't want to fight any more. I was a zombified husk.

Then Justt-K, my best friend and an inspirational human, humoured me with a request: I asked him to call me by a new name. No rhyme or reason, not even to role-play something like we used to. I just felt I needed to try something new. 'Okay, Jade <3' came the Telegram message at 10.30 p.m. on a Thursday night in May 2017.

I smiled again. I almost cried. That feeling of being seen as a woman, shamelessly, fearlessly, even just by one person on a different continent, came back. My fire returned, and has blazed brighter since.

Jade is only one part of my name. Samara-Jade Sendek is the full fruit salad. Sendek was originally a pen name. I took it as my surname because I felt more for it than the one I was born with. No doubt I pissed my parents off, but it's my name and my gender euphoria. They got in the way, so they don't have a say. Simple.

The rest of my name comes from two characters: Samara, from *The Ring*, and Jade, from *Mortal Kombat*. They're not normal beginnings for a trans woman, but bear with me here. People tend to take names of significance when choosing something personal. (I imagine there's a *Buffy* fan named Willow grimacing right now.) For me, my trans story starts with empathy. I felt understood by these women: Jade being a loyal friend, ready to face the impossible, and Samara being a shunned loner in life with no real understanding of who she was or why things happened to her.

An autism diagnosis only answered a part of the experience I'd had growing up. Hindsight being what it is, what with liking shows for girls and princess dresses. My parents pointed me to woodworking and toy swords. Again, I didn't pay it no mind. My brothers from another mother were good company and kept me out of trouble. That's it, though: don't pay it – the 'something's up' voice – no mind.

I found solace in video games. My parents handed me

things like *Command & Conquer* and *Space Marine*. I didn't pay it no mind – the graphics were pretty, and I was an angry kid. When I picked something out, it was the *Elder Scrolls* or *Mass Effect*. I played a woman when I thought nobody was looking. Judgement was a given. 'Someone's getting in touch with his feminine side,' my mother would tease.

When I got my hands on *Mortal Kombat* though, my family expected I'd play someone like Shao Kahn. They saw me playing burly white men in the games they handed me. Shao Kahn was a burly white man. Jade, however, caught my eye. I thought the sexualisation was tacky, but the idea that there was a tanned woman who was every bit the equal of everyone else got me.

Jade was my first 'Oh wow… that's… me' moment. Everyone has those moments, right? Who doesn't want to be a martial-arts babe like Jade? Could I have been like her one day? Sassy and well spoken? Stern and kind?

Naturally, the only thing to do was repress the thought and never speak of it again.

Then at the tender age of fifteen, I was legally allowed to watch horror movies. For extra effect, I saw *The Ring* on a VHS system. I lived in a parochial Australian town, so working VHS players were not too hard to find. Once we shut the blinds and had our popcorn, on came the spook show. The real horror wasn't a vengeful ghost crawling out of a television set from a cursed videotape to kill people. Spooky, yes; terrifying, hell no. The real horror was being understood. A girl being left to fend for herself against forces she has no real understanding of that dominate her life, shunned by people around her and murdered because of it.

Naturally, the only thing to do was repress the thought and never speak of it again.

I hope any readers understand that this was the wrong way to go about things. Deny, repress, act out, do as you please: it all comes bubbling up in the end. I could wax poetical about the human condition, but it's called 'toxic' masculinity for a reason. Getting off it let me think clearer, and soothed my myriad mental conditions.

I've had psychiatrists and armchair psychoanalysts try to unpick my mind. Gender dysphoria is evident. I'll wear a tee and jeans and carry on. People notice my smile when I'm wearing my favourite dresses and coats.

They also pick up a weird danger sense. 'You have knives under your skin,' someone from my local war-gaming group once said. I smiled when I saw that, with no small amount of pride.

The shell of nihilism I built predicated itself on being the biggest threat in the room. Someone could look at me and know that if they tried anything, they'd bleed for it. Anything I did was behind a chilly poker face. If they said something untoward, I'd fire back. My own little terror-bubble. It comes with the territory of wanting to make a career out of punching people.

I liked this part of me. Martial arts is seen as a masculine pursuit; same with things like brewing and war-gaming. A fringe benefit of training early is that my dysmorphia – the part of dysphoria that says, 'Ew, ew, ew, get this misshapen tentacle off me!' – went from discomforting to vague presence. My broad shoulders were battering rams. My thin hips were easier to grapple with. Nobody suspected my twiggy thighs had enough force to launch someone off their feet.

'But those are manly things and I don't like them!'

I imagine every trans woman has a little ten-year-old girl in varying degrees of outspokenness somewhere in their head. That voice in me was quiet. Those paying attention might correctly link her to my 'don't pay it no mind' above. There's a German Bundeswehr motto that sums her up: *Lerne leide ohne zu klagen.* Learn to suffer without complaint. She didn't complain about the healthy parts of masculinity I took, or the toxic parts I discarded. She's patient. She'll try anything once.

When I took to femininity, she spoke up. When I painted my nails, did something nice with my hair, or worked with my artist friends on something, she noticed. Those things she approved of. She didn't care when I traded my soft pastel tops for boots and chains. She screamed when I thought of selling some old training equipment.

The only times that voice uttered dissent was when I wanted to give something up. She was vehement that I wouldn't give up martial arts or metal-band merchandise. These were things I wanted to embrace, to make my own. She didn't complain when I gave up ball sports, woodworking or manual labour. Heaven forbid I give up war-gaming or brewing.

That rascally tomboy phantom knows what she wants. Show her frills and a leotard, and you'll likely get a dry retch in response. She points at witchcraft, technology, blood and thunder.

Witchcraft, even on a superficial level, was an outlet for me to explore femininity. Buddhism and Christianity weren't doing it for me, not with rampant misogyny in the pages. When I started transitioning, I scoffed as I read those 'witchy' social-media bios while sipping tisanes. Wicca beliefs were more than pointy hats and pentagrams. Even so, I kept herbs and celebrated solstices. Little did I know I was practising women's business. For those playing at home, women's roles within an Aboriginal Australian mob.

I am Aboriginal Australian by heritage. I was born white-skinned and raised in White Australian society. Even today, there's still not a whole lot I know about the culture of my Aboriginal heritage. British colonists destroyed most of the Palawa nation in the Tasmanian Genocide. I'm not even sure which Uncles and Aunties could help me learn more about my mob. For reference, the shorthand for Uncles and Aunties is 'Elder'. You're called Uncle or Aunty to denote status as a mob's Elder. The Tasmanian Genocide is also under-named the Black War, since (mostly whitefellas) dispute its status as a genocide. For all intents and purposes, Palawa Aboriginals were annihilated and dispossessed. The only surviving language is Palawa Kani, a pidgin constructed from the mobs' languages. Call a spade a spade: it's a genocide.

I went from witchcraft to learning more about where I came from. Witchcraft substituted for self-exploration. There's only so much a Catholic upbringing teaches you. If your sum experience is an inkblot on a thick 12 x 16 inch canvas, Catholic teaching is a tiny, distant droplet that lands a bit away from that blot. That's not an insult against having your faith. What I'm saying is that there's a whole other lot of ink besides that bit, and basing your waking hours on that drop of a drop felt... restrictive, in a word.

It wasn't until May of 2020 that I had a word for what I was in Aboriginal Australian society: sistergirl. Someone assigned male at birth who takes on feminine roles within the mob. To my relief, there was a word for assigned-female people going to masculine roles: brotherboys. (I've yet to discover non-binary roles. I keep hoping I'll find one.) Fighting, hunting and heavy lifting are usually reserved for men in most Aboriginal Australian mobs. Even now, I wouldn't be a good sistergirl: I backchat. Caregiving isn't my strong suit. I live for a good scrap, verbal or physical. Bush tucker is still something that eludes me.

On the other hand, I'm a storyteller by trade. If I don't have a tool on me, I'll make one. Cooking became fun in a strange way. I'm still not clear on which gender had what roles in my mob, let alone how sistergirls were treated. It all changes depending on where you go. For the most part, the Braiakaulung mob, whose lands I grew up on, were pretty good about non-restrictive roles. Stories taught to kids around me were ones everyone could hear.

Try not to take this as reinforcement of the binary. My experience is more, 'Eh? Just do women's business and it's all deadly.' There are some queer kids who don't have it as well as I did. The mobs I grew up around didn't bat an eyelid when I said I still had an interest in martial arts; some men didn't bat an eyelid when I said I wasn't interested in them.

Others, especially the ones who have traditional views of sexuality and gender, didn't take it well. Fighting is still men's business. I have a girlfriend and an agender partner at the time of writing. It's against the sistergirl expectations in most mobs. I should find a husband and take more homely roles. It stings having those standards thrust upon me, especially when an elder says it.

That rascal in me won't let any of it go without a fight.

It is these experiences that I take to my day job as a narrative designer. There I strive to write 'truth': quintessential, unspoken kernels of understanding. When I came out, writing was easier; getting it seen became the tricky part.

It's my 'truth' that I'm a fighter, that I carry scars from a less-than-ideal rearing, that lace and pastels aren't for me. It's my 'truth' that I'm an unrepentant queer, and that rage is sacrosanct in a society of toxic stoicism. Empathy is punk in the day of the sardonic.

Living as you in performative society is always demanding. Unmanaged expectations can chafe you. If there's one takeaway I want people to understand, it's to find the roads you want to travel. That's it, that's the message: find your own way. Labels are labels. Expectations don't suit everyone. They never agreed with me.

I encourage any readers to do a bit of homework with Jacques Derrida on genre and deconstructive thinking. The simplified version is that the labels you wear, the clique you walk in and the clothes on you denote your genre. Traits hinting to what you are, not 'where you belong'.

I'm a fighter. A brewer. Aboriginal. Trans. Lesbian. Goth. Writer. Game developer. Historian. My 'genres', not comfy boxes someone packages me in. Those paths agreed with who I was.

What makes me a woman is my word. What makes me a fighter is my vocation. In a day where Fallon Fox walks the earth, my fists can be as feminine as the dress under my jacket. Because it doesn't matter what gender you are or which tradition says what: a fist in the face hurts.

In some small way, I still feel alien for being a tomboy. In another, I know it's all internalised. Some dear, trans women friends are breathtakingly beautiful. Non-binary, agender, trans men... all of them live a beauty I feel I'm pantomiming.

I know it's internalised because it's someone else's standards.

I have a voice that's mine. That quiet rascal wants to brew kombucha and beer, so I do. She wants to wear pragmatic coats and dresses, so I do. The spaces I was with before, many of whom still remember my deadname, took my transition in stride. I had a place.

That there was even a word for people like me in my heritage was unimaginably relieving. At least, on some level, I had something more to look forward to than hellfire and brimstone. Aboriginal and Wicca culture had answers when 'polite society' didn't. I may not be the model of femininity to any mob, let alone a model witch, but I wasn't hated for the crime of existence.

Those eddies became the truth I lived. My euphoria was my truth, living as a woman, an artisan, and as the friend I needed years ago. My ideals weren't refined ladies or society's definition of femininity. And power to you if it's your way: I have no desire to slag your smiles. It wasn't for me.

My way is in Boudicca, Tomyris and Grace O'Malley. It is in Lady, Raven and Kerillian. In history and in art, I felt understood. Without Justt-K's nudge, I don't think I'd have taken the plunge. Without the friends I made after coming out, I wouldn't be writing this. And without my housemate, I wouldn't have the words to write this.

I could have transitioned fully feminine. Kept stealthy. Maybe salvaged a sliver of the privilege card I enjoyed while living as a cishet man. But I chose to live my truth:

A hard-rocking, hell-fighting, skull-thumping, wisecracking, whiskey-slugging lady of Australia.

The Empowering Magic of Affirming ID

Laura Kate Dale

When I look back over the timeline of my gender transition, I sometimes forget just how large a gap in time there was between my starting to socially transition and finally getting help, support and acknowledgement from the medical establishment. The wait for assessments, second opinions, hormones, surgery and legal letters felt like an eternity while I was in the thick of it, but in the years since that waiting, time has sort of melted away into the mist of the past a little.

When you're living through it, medical and legal gatekeeping as a trans person feels like it's your whole world, and in many ways it is. Parts of your life seem to be placed on hold, all at the whims of an underfunded and overstretched system of doctors who get to decide how you feel. Life becomes a weird limbo, and that comes with a lot of areas where you have to just sit around, only half living your life.

In the grand scheme of things, the years I spent in that limbo were unpleasant and unnecessarily dragged out, but they passed. Looking back, they feel almost like a bad dream, washed away by breaking free and getting to get on with living my life.

Still, those years spent in limbo were important, and while they were often a source of anxiety and fear, they were also home to one of the most empowering and euphoric times in my life.

I was living socially and professionally under the name Laura long before it was legally my name. As early as my late teens I was exclusively going by the name Laura when spending time with my friends, regardless of how I was outwardly presenting that day, and my earliest unpaid steps into professional writing under the name Laura came years before I had even come out to certain elements of my extended family. Laura was who I was to the people who mattered. But when you're living life under a dual identity, there are complications.

When travelling to comic conventions with friends, we used to rotate over time who would be responsible for booking our shared hotel room, and everyone else would pay them back as the event got closer. Every time that it was my responsibility to book a hotel, I would have to sheepishly ask my friends to wait to one side while I got us booked in, just because I didn't want to have to use my old name in front of them when booking in. Doing so also necessitated a certain degree of downplaying how femme I dressed in situations I knew I might need to show ID, for fear that hotel staff might query my appearance compared to the short-haired teenage boy pictured on my driving licence.

I was lucky: my friends were really understanding of the situation and my discomfort around how things sometimes had to play out. One year I booked us a hotel room, and for goodness knows what reason the hotel decided to have 'Welcome Mr Dale' appear in big letters on the room's TV every time we entered the room. My friends said nothing about it, and I hugely appreciate them for that, but every time I had to see it pop up on the screen, I felt a little less valid as one of the girls.

However, the issues were more notable in my professional life, where I was trying to establish myself as a writer. In the first few months I had been writing more seriously online, I had quietly and perhaps naively assumed that I could keep my status as a trans woman a quiet secret, something I didn't have to talk about. I was writing online from home, I wasn't getting paid, so nobody was going to see me in person, or need to see ID or my banking details. Writing was a hobby I could do quietly under my new identity. It meant I couldn't really show my writing accomplishments to family members I wasn't yet out to, but for the most part it should be fine. That didn't really pan out long term.

Put simply, my writing career got serious faster than I was really prepared for. I got my first little bits of paid work doing super-short reviews of video games for a magazine a few months in, and around the same time started getting invited to travel on press trips, sometimes even outside the country, which often necessitated booking travel or accommodation on my behalf. It quickly became clear if I wanted to keep writing, my birth name and gender marker were going to have to appear on paperwork, and that information wasn't going to stay secret for ever. So I decided to just be open about it. I was going to have to address it from time to time, so why hide it?

For the most part, those I interacted with in the video-game industry were really respectful of the awkward situation I had found myself in and were understanding of the tightrope I was walking. Nobody ever made it a problem for my hotel bookings and invoices to be under a different name from my listings on front-facing paperwork, but it was never any less uncomfortable to me on an individual level. When an editor at a magazine starts filling out information to book a flight and you have to correct them to change the name you use to a name you have not used in years that feels nothing like you, it can be really heartbreaking.

I had been living as Laura for years. I was a woman, and had been living openly as such for years. Every time I had to tell someone my deadname while booking into a hotel, or show them ID from my more masculine years to prove my identity, it felt like I was tearing away a piece of the identity I had spent those years working to establish. It enforced this horrible feeling that Laura was a performance I was enacting, one to be stripped away when it was time to establish my actual identity. It made it tough not to feel that my status as a woman was something that might just be taken away from me at a moment's notice.

Every time I had to show someone my old information, something happened I could never take back: that person saw a legal document saying who I was, and I was placed in a box in their head I desperately wanted to avoid.

Getting your name or gender marker changed on ID isn't inherently a part of being valid as a trans person. In hindsight, I was just as valid as a woman when I was having to hand over that old ID as I am today. Getting your ID updated as a trans person can be a messy, time-consuming, expensive process, full of legal and medical gatekeeping, and for many it's a difficult road to get through. I know it took me years, and during that time I was doing my best to keep on living my life as normal. Getting an updated ID wasn't what made my transition real, but it made it feel real.

It took me a fair few years to be able to get my passport updated to list me as Laura, and female. I held off on changing my name by deed poll or changing my passport photo until I could change my gender marker too, and that needed two doctors to sign off that they both agreed I was trans. I had to get started on hormones and get a letter saying my transition wasn't going to be reversed in my lifetime in order to make sure that when I renewed my passport it would list me as Laura and a woman. The thought of listing me as Laura, who was male, somehow felt worse than seeing 'male' next to my deadname.

It was a long time coming, but on a bright sunny morning in the summer of 2014, my new passport arrived. It was perfect. It was me. It was a legal document that validated who I was, in a way that was hard to deny for outsiders.

On paper, getting my passport updated didn't change much about how I lived my life. I was still Laura to my friends; I was still writing as Laura. I was finally able to change my name and gender marker at my day job, but, day to day, having a new passport didn't change much of my daily routine or overall life plans. What it did do, however, was replace years of hesitance and anxiety around my identity with a new-found sense of confidence. That was a truly euphoric experience.

When travelling to events with friends, I didn't feel any need to tone down my appearance to line it up with someone who had not existed for many years just to deal with a hotel employee. When invoicing for work, I didn't have to dance around how to best put my name on paperwork. When travelling, I didn't have to travel as one person and get changed part way through my journey.

As someone who loves aircraft, and for a few years did a lot of flying and international travelling for work, I vividly remember the first international flight I got to take with my new passport, flying from London to Los Angeles for the 2015 E3 video game convention. In the years prior to this, I'd always had to do this awkward dance when travelling: presenting masculine while going through security and during the journey; getting out the other end of the terminal, then quickly performing an awkward outfit change in an airport bathroom from my hand luggage before meeting whoever I was meeting the other end of my flight.

Getting to stroll up to security as myself and pass all these physical and metaphorical identity checkpoints without hassle was a truly validating experience. Every time someone official looked at my photo, looked at my name, looked at my face and allowed me to pass, it felt like they were confirming that yes, this was definitely who I was. Every step of the way I felt more and more comfortable, knowing that if airport-level security accepted that this was who I was, there wasn't too much chance of anyone else quibbling my identity. I had made it through some of the theoretically strictest examinations of identity there are, and had been seen as myself.

I sat down on that plane grinning from ear to ear. It felt like the beginning of a new chapter in my life. I clutched my ticket tight in my hand. I could go anywhere and do anything as me.

Beyond that, a lot of the moments where having an updated ID felt most empowering were moments that I didn't even have to show it to anyone. It was the moments where I knew I could show it if I needed to. I knew I had something to protect me in situations that had previously been sources of anxiety.

Going to use the changing rooms in a clothing shop? If they tried to send me to the men's changing area, I had ID I could use to stand my ground. The same for going swimming or doing sports; if someone tried to assert I was in the wrong gendered space, I had a government-issued document that said this was the correct space for me to use. When using public bathrooms, if someone tried to hassle me, I had a legal document that showed I was in the right.

Where I had spent years standing in bathroom queues imagining escape routes if someone tried to hassle me, now I quietly imagined showing them my passport and calmly sorting the situation out smoothly. It completely changed how I felt when living my life out in public.

Now, I would be foolish to assume that if someone wanted to be intensely transphobic, my ID was going to stop them. There would still be people who would give me a hard time, or try to tell me I didn't belong as a woman, but, if nothing else, I knew I would have a legal leg to stand on. That was enough. It felt like a suit of armour. It was a first line of defence. If someone told me I wasn't a woman, I could defend myself and my rights. For the first time, I felt safe defending my gender to the world.

If someone decided to call the police on me for peeing in the women's bathroom, I'd be able to show I was legally in the right place. It was some form of safety I could tangibly carry with me as I lived my life.

In the years since getting my passport updated, I've had it on my person basically every single day without fail. It's a little piece of security. It's the knowledge that I am Laura, I am a woman, and I can prove that fact if pressed on it by someone trying to push me out of womanhood. Getting my ID updated didn't change much of my day-to-day life, but it made me feel so much more valid and safe telling the world loudly who I am.

Epidermis: Tattoos and Transmasculine Selfhood

Emmett Nahil

Twenty-five, Arab-American writer and editor based on the
East Coast, who loves horror, retro media and art history

The epidermis is a thin, superficial layer of skin. It is the
most immediate layer, visible at any point on the body.
Functions of the epidermis include touch sensation and
protection against microorganisms, and it is comprised of
five distinct layers.

When people ask about my childhood, I respond very
earnestly that I do not have very many memories of my
young life. Whether it was the lack of memorable events,
or the overabundance of an active inner imagination, I
mostly remember things in images, pictures and shades
of light. I went to school in my coastal, profoundly Irish-
Italian suburban town, lived in my parents' house with my
sibling, and visited my father's parents on Cape Cod for
long weekends and summer vacation.

I remember being seven and looking upwards, through
my grandparents' glass table, and seeing their fancy plates
stacked on the shelf through the glass, the surface warping

and contorting the design. I'm not sure if I just remember that because they still have the plates, however. The image in my mind could just be my imagination, solidified through time and through external confirmation: yes this exists, because we still have the table. The plates still have the same design, and you didn't imagine that. You couldn't have.

Stratum corneum: The outer layer, composed of the many skin cells that the human body sheds into the environment – as a result, these cells are found in dust throughout the home. Helps repel water and debris.

In my lifetime, my father's parents have lived in an apartment in the city, and then back in a house on Cape Cod again, and then in a too-big house north of the city. These are the facts of their life, of our family's life, but I remember the locations differently, and mostly via kitchen tables. The apartment house, through the glass table. The Cape house I remember through the dented and well-worn kitchen table, always laden with straight runners and perfectly matched place mats to prevent my sibling and me from smearing it with crayon or Magic Marker. The most recent house's kitchen table was much finer, ensconced in a dining room, with fancy place settings laid out in advance. Appearances, such as they were, have always been important to them.

My grandfather and my father would sit at the dining-room table and talk over drinks every time we visited.

We'd clear the tables, and they'd sit and talk for as long as they needed. I'd always wanted to be included, to be a part of my grandfather's rambling stories and funny jokes about whatever the hell they'd decided to go on about that night. The dark amber-brown of the table coloured that memory warm and welcoming.

The unhappy opposite of my penchant for visual memory is unfortunate, but just as accurate. I remember the bad things visually too. Fights and traumas, little nicks and pieces chopped out of memory, dents in perception that don't heal so easily.

Stratum lucidum: A durable layer of dead skin cells is found only on the palms of the hands, fingertips and the soles of the feet.

I remember being a teenager, in the second Cape house, sitting at the table. My fingers fiddled with an intricately patterned, plastic-coated place mat, and I casually told my father and grandfather after dinner that I wanted tattoos. I did my best to slip it in to the conversation like dropping a tiny pebble into surf: gently, smoothly, so that the comment wouldn't send out too many ripples. The less splash the better, I figured. Understandably, I'd always seen my grandfather as a humane, warm and funny person; he'd never given me reason to not think so. He was a conservative, mostly retired businessman, an Armenian-Lebanese gentleman and storyteller who'd lived in Massachusetts his whole life, and who felt strongly and fervently about a great number of things. There was so much of my own father in him, and what I saw in my father I saw in myself, although I didn't have the words or the self-awareness to recognise it at the time.

I don't remember the exact words that he said in response to my statement, but I do recall the twist of rage on his face immediately after I said it. It was a contortion I'd never really had cause to see on him before. I don't remember his words, other than the knowledge that they were angry, went on for a long time, and cut at a part of me I did not have the tools to comprehend.

It was a long talk, and I remember sidling back upstairs, into bed, to the spare room that I shared with my sibling in my grandparents' house, and feeling the hot swell of anger and shame roll over me. I remember feeling that my body wasn't my own. I remember being able to hear the distant crash of waves from an open window, even in the darkness.

Stratum granulosum: The layer where part of keratin production occurs. Keratin is a protein that is the main component of skin.

I had always liked how tattoos looked. I'd grown up looking at the covers on my father's seemingly unending record collection, picking through dusty cover after cover of old-school punk albums, classic rock LPs and post-punk collections. I'd poke through his CDs, opening up the jewel cases and looking through the leaflets, seeing pictures of band members posturing and posing in a way that let easy confidence and hard-edged grit roll out of the photos. I didn't want to play an instrument per se, although I'd tried. I was after the look, the high-octane self-assuredness that came through in their clothes, the rough haircuts and the tattoos many of them sported. The sense of confidence was what was attractive, was what was cool as hell.

At the time I was more of a kid than a proper teenager. I hadn't grown into the lackadaisical mutiny of late adolescence, and at any rate, I didn't conceive of an urge to change my physical form as rebellion. To me, changing my appearance was a method of finding a form of embodiment that suited me best, of self-decoration that might be a magic charm that would allow me to feel at home in my body. That kind of mystical ward wouldn't be for anyone but myself, in the end.

After all, if upsetting my family was truly my goal, I would have kept quiet, I reasoned to myself. I loved them, and I didn't want to shock or surprise them too much. Sharing these things was, and still is, a kindness; a way of forewarning those I love of what's in my heart, what I'm electing to do. Even then I felt quite grown-up and was prone to doing things on my own without telling anyone at all. If I was going to be independent and do what I wanted to do anyway, forewarning them was an act of trust. But intent doesn't equal effect, and the long shadow of that conversation stayed with me, despite my younger self not quite understanding why.

*

Stratum spinosum: A layer that gives the skin strength as well as flexibility.

I remember thinking about what my grandfather's face must have looked like when he learned about me being a boy. My parents graciously did the honours, and I imagined it must've looked similar to that night, twisted up in something close to rage. Maybe with a healthy dollop of confusion, for good measure.

The thing about living as a minority is that the goal of assimilation worms its way into your brain in insidious ways. You learn to develop a healthy sense of rage and confusion whenever one of your own refuses to assimilate: into gender designated at birth, into whiteness, into a comfortable sense of lower-middle-class gratitude. It becomes the only acceptable way to achieve happiness in a context that's inherently in opposition to who you are, to your very identity.

Refusal to assimilate correctly became the norm for me. The possibility of being enveloped into a white, cis majority was never an acceptable path in regards to my own gender. Even if I was interested in working hard to achieve my grandfather's version of success through ethnic assimilation, my transness would bar me from ever fully completing that process and merging into the majority. As I saw things, I either was a girl or was not, and since I was not, there was to be no aspiration to cis-ness. No other options remained. There's been a lot of ink spilled on the nature of dysphoria, on the ways and means in which transgender folks experience pain in America, on the opposition we face in the pursuit of living our full lives. I've felt that weight, and nothing my family could do or say could match what America has already done. You'll forgive me if I skip over that particular painful part in favour of the more interesting bits. Pain on the outside is simply easier and more cinematic than pain on the inside.

The epidermis is, mostly, a protective barrier. It holds in the dermis, and after that, the rest of your body's veins, muscles, nerves, organs. The ink that you get when you're tattooed is shot directly through the needle and into the dermis, that second, denser layer of skin, and once the ink pools in place, your body sends white blood cells to trap and contain the colour inside the body. It thinks the material is an invading sickness. In order to protect your organs, the delicate bloody mass that comprises your body, it forms fine lines, delicate dot-work and dense black shadows. They may stretch and dull and age with time, but the ink stays there until your skin is no more.

I graduated high school, and got my first professional tattoo the day after my eighteenth birthday. I picked out a thick-lined, American traditional-style cobra that stretched the length of my side. I decided on something poisonous, something totemic that wasn't easily touched or held on to. Something you wouldn't want as a pet. My reasoning wasn't the clearest, to be sure, but I'd thought that it must be better to get my first tattoo on the most painful part of my body, so that everything else afterwards would be easy.

I went by myself, taking the Red Line train to the appropriate stop and getting more and more nervous as I walked down the block, up the narrow steps to the small second-floor studio. The artist I went to was a jovial New Jersey Latina named Suze, who made sure the stencil was placed just the way I wanted it and didn't poke too much fun at me when I told her I'd just listened to Biggie's 'Ready to Die' for the first time last week.

In more ways than one, a tattoo artist is a lot like a good bartender: ready to meet your needs, talkative insomuch as you want to hold a conversation, and with a ready assemblage of interesting stories if the conversation grows slack. I found out that Suze had been at the same Panic! at the Disco reunion show I'd gone to last month, and incessantly reminded me to take water breaks. She didn't question my choices or ask too many questions about why I wanted the tattoo she was giving me. She didn't point out the fact that after a while I was actively wincing in pain from the motion of the needle. The snake tattoo touched the length of my torso, from my upper ribs to the top of my hip bone, and it hurt like a road rash or graze that had been sitting out in the sun to burn. I left raw, bloodied, my side wrapped in plastic wrap and masking tape, and with endorphins rushing through me. I was incredibly, incandescently happy.

That same year I met the first other transmasculine person I'd ever known. As it turns out, tattoos also help convince your doctor that you have a good enough pain tolerance to self-inject hormones.

*

Stratum basale: Where the skin's most important cells, called keratinocytes, are formed before moving to the surface of the epidermis and being shed into the environment. This layer also contains melanocytes, the cells that are largely responsible for determining the colour of our skin and protecting it from the harmful effects of UV radiation.

Tattoos on skin have the convenient and highly pragmatic ability to dissuade curiosity about the body beneath. They help you exist as a person whose body is interesting for reasons other than gender divergence. People have been well trained by *Ink Master* and assorted other Bravo reality-television shows to assume that each tattoo must surely have a deep spiritual or emotional significance, and that every one must, in fact, signal a dramatic turn in your very personhood, or commemorate a personal trauma writ large on the skin. I've taken to making up extraordinary stories for each one, depending on who's asking. According to three different accounts, the dagger and number on my right forearm means alternatively that I've won in three knife fights, was a member of a cultic blood pact, or have survived three different attacks on my life. A straight face and compelling cliffhanger tends to be distracting.

The distraction can be a lifeline, a way of showing your colours and affiliating yourself with certain aesthetics. To me, the aesthetics and presentation of having tattoos bring gender home. They act as an anchor to my skin, holding me down and protecting my insides when the entirety of my body simultaneously feels like too much and not enough.

After a certain point, you stop counting the number of tattoos and piercings you have. Whenever folks ask, I have to do a quick mental once-over, and scan my own body in my mind's eye to make sure I count correctly. Ensuring all the parts are there can be difficult, and sometimes it's as easy as sitting down at a table.

Dermis: Underneath the epidermis lies the dermis, which contains: blood vessels that carry oxygen and rise to the surface to fight infection, nerves that help us relay signals coming from the skin, various glands, hair follicles, and collagen, a protein that is responsible for giving skin strength and elasticity.

If you don't mind keeping a secret, I can tell you that the reality is that people ask fewer questions about what's going on in your pants if they're distracted by what you've got drawn on your arms. Elaborate performance combined with a kind of camouflage can let any creature survive in an environment oppositional to its very existence. The need to adapt is constant, but the manner in which you choose to do it can be a deep wellspring of affirmation.

I don't have anyone's name or face inked on me. My body is mine in its entirety, anchored by the adaptive art that's been placed on my skin. When I stretch and my shirt rides up, I'm not worried about being asked about the scars on my chest, because of the protection of the broad black and grey pieces spanning my sides. The totem I'd hoped for that first day at Suze's shop still lies on the outside of my skin to watch over me, a patron saint of my father's record-store icons. They're more powerful than anything I could say about myself in words, because people judge on looks and remember you with their eyes more than their brains. I did wind up getting another piece on my other side, and it was just as uncomfortable as Suze's first snake.

I still have to correct my grandfather about my name and my pronouns every so often, and I still have trouble with my memory. I can live with that. As it turns out, ripping off the Band-Aid, getting the pain over with, does not guarantee that anything will get easier with time. It doesn't preclude further discomfort. The picture is what matters, after all.

Subcutaneous tissue: The deepest layer of the skin is called the subcutaneous layer, the subcutis, or the hypodermis. Like the dermis, the layer contains blood vessels and nerves.

Importantly, the subcutis contains a layer of fat, which acts as a cushion against physical trauma to internal organs, muscles and bones. Additionally, the body will turn to this fat in times of starvation to provide power to its various processes.

*

Quite recently, on a visit to my parents' house, my father announced that he was considering getting a tattoo. When I asked what he wanted, he grinned and proudly pulled up a few artists that he'd looked into, ones nearby whose style he liked, handing his phone over to me to take a look.

As tattoos age, the ink settles deeper into the dermis and as the years pass by, your body carries off the pigment. It chips away at the colour and the pattern, but the blacks, the definitive outlines of the image, stay. I sat down with my father at the kitchen table after dinner to talk, but mostly to listen. He still hasn't told me when or where he wants to get his own tattoo, but I know I will be the first to know when he does.

Feeling Safe and Welcome, and Seen by My Teen Idols

Laura Kate Dale

If you want to get an idea of what I was like as a teenager in the mid 2000s, going through an unwanted puberty in the lead-up to my coming out as a trans woman, I was basically the aesthetic poster child for the emo music scene. Pretty much all my clothing was black, with occasional splashes of red thrown in to accentuate. I had grown my hair out and dyed it black. Everything I wore was so skinny-fit it took me a considerable amount of time to get dressed in the morning. Belts, wristbands and jackets were covered in spikes. I was a ball of angst and confusion without much clue where to direct those feelings.

In hindsight, it's clear why I was struggling. I was living with – at the time undiagnosed – autism, and I didn't yet know that being trans was at the core of my discomfort with testosterone puberty. I lacked routine, I felt different and strange, I was socially isolated, and my body was changing in ways I couldn't control. It was a really confusing and scary time in my life, and I latched onto a subculture that in many ways focused on creating a sense of community for lonely, depressed teens.

But when I think back to those years in my life, the thing that really kept me afloat was music, and discovering my own taste in music for the first time.

As a teen, the bands I really found myself gravitating towards listening to were angry, raw and emotionally charged. There was a lot of rock and punk of varying stripes, but the bands that stuck with me most always offered some sense of understanding and community around being in a state of emotional turmoil. It was anger and sadness tinged with hope, the idea of getting complex emotions out, then taking a moment to breathe and remember that things are actually going to be okay, and you're not alone.

The two bands that probably meant the most to me as a teen who wasn't yet out as trans were My Chemical Romance and Against Me!. Thankfully, in the decade or more since I was an angsty teen, both bands have not only continued to exist in various shapes and forms, but both have remained acts that I feel explicitly safe to see perform live as a trans person.

Considering how many of my childhood heroes have turned out to be massive transphobes in the years since I idolised their works, it's wonderful to still be able to enjoy some of the creative voices I appreciated in my formative years.

So, firstly, let's talk about My Chemical Romance a little. MCR as a band are pretty well known worldwide, after having some mainstream radio success as well as some controversy around their third album, *The Black Parade*, released back in 2006. The album was a theatrical rock concept album that ultimately built up to a message of hope, with the final track of the album being an anti-suicide anthem about finding the will to stay alive, no matter how alone you feel. It was an album that focused initially on feelings of loss, loneliness and isolation, but used those as a backdrop to build up a message of strength. You might feel lonely and sad, but it's okay, there is a whole army of people out there just like you, and together we will keep living, one day at a time.

Despite the album's perception as a dark and depressing ode to suicide, mainly sparked by some misleading tabloid coverage in the UK blaming a young girl's suicide on the band, My Chemical Romance were always explicit at their live shows about the importance of talking about your feelings and getting help when things get too tough. They would take time in live shows to stop and remind people 'don't suffer alone – get help if you need it; you're not weak for accepting mental health support'. One of my strongest teenage memories of feeling respite from my depression was standing in the crowd at one of their shows, in a crowd of thousands, all belting out 'I'm Not Okay' at the top of our lungs, saying out loud that something was wrong and not pretending it wasn't the case. They were exactly the band I needed as a struggling teen.

My Chemical Romance officially broke up as a band in 2013, but during the years that followed many of the band's members started their own solo careers and continued to tour and make music. During that period of time I came out as trans, got diagnosed as on the autism spectrum, and dealt with a lot of the issues that had been causing the depression that had been a hallmark of my teen years. My life improved a lot, but I still kept a very fond place in my heart for that band and their music. It had been a huge comfort to me at a time when I needed one.

So we skip forward to the year 2015. While My Chemical Romance was no longer a band, their lead singer Gerard Way was doing a solo tour of his own music and was doing a few tour dates in the UK. I'd enjoyed his debut album a lot, and so I camped out overnight to get myself a nice spot front and centre at his first UK tour date.

I was pretty exhausted by the time the show began, due in part to not really getting much sleep camping outside the show venue. As people poured in behind me and the crowd grew more packed, that exhaustion all faded away. I was really excited to get a chance to see the voice of my teenage angst perform, from a perfect spot on the centre of the barrier.

The show itself was amazing, but what I really remember from that night was a single moment between two songs. Way stopped singing and just took a moment to thank any trans people who had felt safe enough to come along to the show that night.

'I know there are people out there who can say it

better than me, but if you're here tonight and you are transgender, or you're non-binary, I have so much love for you; thank you for being here and for being you. And if you're here and you're not trans or non-binary, but you have a friend who is and you're good to them, I love you for that.'

Words can't quite do justice to how magical that moment felt: someone whose music had helped me through some of the toughest years of my life stood and made it clear that I and people like me were welcome at his shows. The crowd erupted in cheers of support, and I just felt incredibly at home.

So often, for a trans person, crowded events with lots of people can be daunting. There are concerns about personal safety to consider, and any crowd large enough will probably contain someone transphobic just by the law of large numbers. But to stand in a room of thousands and feel safe and wanted and accepted was an incredibly powerful feeling. It really meant a lot to me.

Winding back a little, let's talk a bit about the band Against Me!, whose music was the other constant in those turbulent years before my transition. Against Me! were a much more straightforward punk band in terms of their sound, with a charismatic singer who was hard not to get swept up in. The band's music focused on themes of standing up to authority, refusing to conform, and taking time for self-reflection and understanding. Again, as a trans person who wasn't yet out and needed a boost of confidence to face the fact she didn't want to be who she was expected to be, I really found a lot to connect with in the music of Against Me! in my teenage years.

However, it was a few years before I came out, in 2007, that Against Me!'s music touched me in a way I could not shake. It was the year the band released an album called *New Wave*, and in particular a track called 'The Ocean'.

In that track the lead singer of the band, who would not come out as a trans woman for another five years, spends around four and a half minutes singing about how she wishes she had been born female, how her mother had planned to call her Laura, about the life she imagines she might have lived if she had been born female. As a not-yet-out trans woman, it was an eye-opening experience for me. Here was someone who, like me, had been assigned male at birth, putting words to that secret thought I'd had for years: *I wish I had been born a woman.*

I wasn't ready to join the dots between 'I wish I had been born a woman' and 'I could live as a woman some day, if that is what I want', but that song put the first tentative cracks in my transgender eggshell. It wasn't enough for me to come out then and there, but it certainly got me thinking more frequently about the idea of being a woman. That song carried me along through a good few years, and when I finally came out, it was a really powerful source of strength.

The band's lead singer, Laura Jane Grace, came out as trans in 2012, and two years later the band released an album titled *Transgender Dysphoria Blues*, a punk album full of raw, angry tracks about the pain, fury and beauty of living life visibly and unapologetically trans. Needless to say, I felt incredibly seen. That album, to this day, is still one I come back to in times of hardship, when I need an energy boost. It's full of tracks that energise me, that give me the strength to fight on in difficult days.

Fast forward to 2016, and I got to see Against Me! perform live in London, in a little 1,500 person venue hidden away in Camden. No words can quite do justice to how amazingly affirming it was to attend that show. Again, I camped out early to get a good spot up on the front barrier, and as the band came on stage, the room erupted in joyous energy. There was a confident, beautiful trans woman on that stage, singing at the top of her lungs about her lived experiences, and the entire room was singing along. That room was filled with other trans people like me, whose experiences had been put to words, screaming in unison and camaraderie. We were together. We were safe. We were the majority in that room. Our experiences were not just being heard: they were the narrative of the room. Everyone was here to share, listen to, and be a part of a night dedicated to trans stories.

A lot of people I grew up idolising as creators turned out to be really shitty people. I tend to live life these days assuming that any piece of media I consume might have been created by a secret transphobe, unless stated otherwise. I was much more optimistic and idealistic as a teen, and even if most of the bands I grew up listening to turned out to be kind of trash, I love that at least two musicians that helped me through my angsty emo years turned out to be people I could continue to enjoy as an out trans adult.

I'm glad, because there's nothing quite as euphoric as feeling explicitly at home in a crowd of thousands.

Transition in Lockdown: Shaving and Growth

William Keohane

Twenty-four, writer, currently pursuing an MA in Creative Writing

For as long as I can remember, my dad has had a beard. He looks like the man he is, like an Irishman; he's built sturdy, with strong arms and legs and a round middle. He has thick black (greying) hair. At Christmas, my friends always loved being around him. He's like Santa Claus! Angie would tell me whenever we were playing at the house after school. He was jolly, too; when he laughed the room would shake. We would all laugh with him.

And when I was a baby, a toddler, a young child, he would tell me: You used to love the feel of my beard against your face. The story goes, according to him, that when he would come home from work, I would run to the door and greet him: Beard me, Daddy! He would rub his face against mine so I could feel the soft scratch of tangled bristles.

At twenty-three, when I told him what I needed to do with my life to be happy, to stay alive, and asked him and my mom to offer me a new name, he put his arms around me. I felt the familiar scratch of his beard on my face.

You know I'll always love you. I'll always be proud of you. No matter what.

My dad told me once that he was self-conscious about his grey beard, how it doesn't match his hair or eyebrows. I would joke with him whenever the ad for Just For Men hair dye flashed across the television. I could get you some of that, Pop, if you like? In the advert, a daughter brings her father the box of dye, and they smile at each other in the eerie way that paid performers always do. People who have probably only just met each other, probably want to leave the set as soon as they can, and are clearly overacting.

A few years later, I'm no longer his daughter, but we still share the joke. In the pharmacy, any time I go to pick up my prescription of testosterone, needles and circular Band-Aids, I scan the aisles for hair dye. I search for him, for our shared history, for familiarity.

On the couch in my parents' living room they spoke the name William into the open air, and it landed on me. Settled deep into my bones.

Then began the process of telling our extended family. Aunts, uncles, cousins, friends. My Aunt Cassie was the only person who responded with wholehearted acceptance and love. No questions. Everyone else had questions.

When I had to travel abroad for top surgery, because the only surgeon in the country who would do the procedure retired last year, I stayed with Cassie for three weeks. She drove me to and from the clinic, helped me dress the bandages, held me in a soft hug when I cried from pain at the post-op assessment. She checked on me every four hours to make sure I wasn't in too much pain, to make sure I was keeping food down.

Six months after surgery, in the July heat, the first summer of a pandemic that has made travel abroad impossible, I cannot visit Cassie in person; I cannot hug her with my healed chest. Instead, I send a card to her home in Toronto to thank her. She video-calls me, teary-eyed, marvelling at my changing voice and features. I'm half a year on testosterone, half a year with a new chest. How lucky I am to have been able to receive gender-affirming healthcare abroad, right before the world came to a standstill. How lucky I am to have a woman like her in my life. An aunt, an ally, a friend.

When my mom finally told my grandfather, an eighty-year-old farming man living in rural Canada, he only had one question for her. So, should I call him Will or William?

I don't have an answer for him. I love both.

My Irish grandmother died in the middle of a cold winter after five years of dementia decline. Maggie raised me as if I was her child. On Saturdays and Sundays I would play at her house; she would take me to Mass, feed me famine food of overboiled turnip, carrots, potatoes. I loved her with all my heart.

My mother, however, had trouble with the fact that I'd often return from Maggie's house in the woods to ours in the city shorn like a sheep. Maggie would cut long strands of my blonde curls off, which I never objected to. In my mind, hair was an inconvenience. My tomboy life was much easier if I could run around without a fringe obscuring my vision, if I could jump into ponds and streams and dry off quickly.

Around the anniversary of her death, my dad and I drove my mom to visit Maggie's headstone. To say hello.

I was a pallbearer at her funeral, along with my dad, my brother, my three cousins. In the West, and in Ireland, pallbearers are often relatives of the dead, usually men. But not at Maggie's funeral. She was a feminist, my dad told us, in the small chapel filled with golden light the day after she died. She would have wanted both men and women involved. She would have wanted it equal. The ground was frozen solid. The six of us carried her gently, concentrating hard on our movements. Trying not to slip, trying to place her, softly, into the earth, into the November snow.

We stand, my father and I, in front of her marbled headstone. It is winter; a year later, it is still a nameless space. A mound of brown earth acts as her blanket.

Hello, Maggie. I miss you. I wanted to let you know that my name is Will now. I hope that's okay with you.

Maggie had insisted I was baptised in the church next to her house, and my agnostic parents were happy to oblige. I was given two girl names, both soft, unique. Both beautiful. But neither one fitted.

I still remember how she would pronounce my old name, the vowel sounds harshened by her nasally drawl. How she would call me for dinner, call me in from the garden, beckon me into the bathroom to wash off the day's collected dirt and grime from under my nails.

I never heard her say the name William.

As my father and I drove away from her resting place, he put his hand on my knee. She would have been absolutely fine with it, you know. She was a traditional Irishwoman, yes, but she was also progressive. Maggie told me once she wished she had been able to become a priest. I couldn't say anything or else the tears would have started to fall, so I simply smiled back at him. I smiled all the way home.

In adolescence, I tried to blend as best I could. I kept my hair long, tied up in a low ponytail. I wore the ankle-length blue skirts, the typical school uniform for teenage girls in the Republic of Ireland, or at least in County Limerick, where I had lived all my life.

I never wore make-up until others put it on me. My body was not my own.

And then college came, and I became myself. I started to find the boy I'd lost along the way. It took some time, but he arrived.

I wanted to cut my hair short, to have the lad haircut typical of young men in my city, in my college. I wanted to blend again, differently this time. Blending in the right direction. When I first went to the hairdresser's with a photo of a cropped men's cut on my phone, the woman at the counter gave me a once-over. Oh sweetie, she said, you don't want that.

I tried going to different barber's shops all week. I'm sorry, they would tell me. We don't cut girls' hair. This I couldn't understand. Surely male and female strands were the same; surely, the fibres of keratin on my head were genderless. Weren't they?

Dejected, I decided to try the one place I thought would be most likely to say no, like all the others. Johnny's Barbers, a short walk from campus, was about as hyper-masculine as they come. The men wore tailored suits while shaving their clients, slapped each other on the asses with damp towels. You could smell the cologne, talcum powder and hair gel from down the road. I called the manager.

Yes, he said. I'll do it for you. But don't tell anyone. This is just the once.

And so it became our shared secret. I went with Sofia, my closest friend, the one person in my life who knows how to calm me down effortlessly. The two of us sat, long-haired and silent, amidst the men on the leather bench. They called me up, shaved off strips of curls, and gave me exactly what I wanted. But don't tell anyone.

After I became William, I had to have my name legally changed. In 2015, along with legalising marriage equality, Ireland introduced the Gender Recognition Act. With a few forms, fees and a trip to the High Courts in Dublin, I could change my name to William and my gender to male. I could have a new birth certificate reissued. In two years I could have a new passport.

Sofia was my witness. She swore on a Bible for me, in front of a solicitor, in the print shop opposite the courthouse.

Do you hereby declare that the aforementioned Mr William Keohane does wholly renounce, relinquish and abandon the use of his old name and in place thereof does assume and adopt from the date hereof his new name. That he may hereafter be called, known and distinguished not by his old name but by his new name, until death.

Yeah, grand, she responded.

We went for pizza afterwards. Came home to my flat and watched *Chalet Girl*, a shitty romcom on Netflix. It was a normal, extraordinary day.

The first formative adult relationship I had started at an amateur drag event on our college campus. I wasn't out yet; I knew myself, in some small way, but I didn't know. Not yet.

Sam was doing make-up for other drag queens there, clearly a pro. I was wearing a blue suit jacket, a shirt, my chest compressed. Sam offered to paint me in boy drag, and I accepted. We sat facing each other and I watched graceful hands move over my face. I stared into blue eyes, long lashes, elegant arched eyebrows. I had to stop myself from grinning, feeling my heartbeat thumping in my throat.

When it was finished, Sam smiled. You look so hot. We started dating three months later.

My first beard, though, came before this. At our formal ball at the end of secondary school, at the splinter between teenhood and adulthood. I was seventeen.

Tom had been my best friend since we were four years old. It was a shared agreement between us that we'd be each other's dates, although he had a girlfriend at the time. We assumed this before we'd even started school. I used to skateboard with him weekly, both of us with our baggy hoodies, both of us with our long, ambiguous hair.

A few nights before the ball, we went out for drinks. I hadn't yet decided what to wear; the prospect of a dress terrified me. But there was no other option. In a Catholic school, all the pretty young homophobes seemed to just be waiting for bait. No one my age came out until college.

That night at the bar, in a drunken haze, I told him: I'm gay.

At this stage he was also several pints deep. I'm not sure I'll be able to remember this in the morning, he responded. So Tom, taking a pen from his pocket, scrawled my disclosure on our drink receipt.

When he came to collect me for the ball later in the week, dressed handsomely in a black tux, Tom took the receipt out of his jacket pocket.

I didn't forget.

Sam and I dated for two years. On the days when I felt low, felt small, felt weak, Sam would take brown mascara and sketch the outline of a beard on my face. Over the soft blonde down, I'd feel myself becoming: When Sam was finished, I'd look at my face through the camera of my phone. I would watch my face in the mirror. I could see someone I wanted to be; I could catch myself in every reflective surface in our flat and smile. Here was a man. Here I was, a man.

There were days when I would shave nothing, just smooth white shaving cream over my cheeks and chin and slide a blade along my face, tracing. A slow glacier moving through valleys.

Now, every two weeks, I inject a small dose of pale amber liquid into my thigh. It is strange to be changing so rapidly while the world is quiet, while I'm mostly alone in my bedroom. When I was able to see friends again, to leave the house, to sit in parks, six feet apart, I liked watching people study the differences. They would often comment on my fluffy cheeks, the small scattering of blonde hairs blooming above my lips.

At home alone, I study myself too.

This body is writing chapters for me; I exist in this year, in this time and space, pounds of flesh heavier than last summer.

I take pictures of this new body – craters on my forehead, wisps of blonde and brunette, a thickening path of down on my stomach – and I think of ways to love it. Small acts of care.

Rub scar cream into the thin red lines on my chest, across the puckered places where pain still twinges. Rub the excess off with a towel, watch the pink pimples blooming. Touch the soft blonde hairs, thickening (I think? I hope) along the crevasse of my pecs. Touch the small garden of freckles on the left side of my chest, next to my nipple. Still there, even after surgery, just in a new location.

In Roman times, boys would rub oil into the skin of their cheeks and chin. These prepubescent men hoped that this would urge beards to grow before their time. I suppose I am doing the same. Lately I find myself rubbing my thumb up against the small golden hairs on my chin, almost as a comfort. Now, seven months on testosterone, I have coarse black hairs on my cheeks to shave, too.

And I do. It is a ritual, almost. I play some music (Kevin Abstract, Frank Ocean, Bon Iver) and I watch my face in the pale blue light of the bathroom. I shave.

I feel like I've always wanted a beard, before I ever had the language to describe myself, my gender. Sometimes I wonder if it's because I want another mask. I ask myself: Do I want a beard because it is symbolic of masculinity? Do I want a beard because it's another thing to hide behind?

And I pick up the razor because I like the man I'm becoming. I don't need to hide him.

Drunken Compliments and Body Positivity in the Club

Laura Kate Dale

For most of my life I have actively avoided nightclubs and late-night venues like the plague. I'm on the autism spectrum, and even on the best of days, the volume, level of crowding and amount of flashing lights can be more than a little overwhelming. Additionally, I just never really got on well with the energy of a lot of high-street nightclub crowds; slightly aggy and rowdy people in their early to mid-twenties have never been the kind of people to make me feel safe, so I largely stayed away.

I knew I could enjoy nights out under the right conditions; I am a big fan of live rock music shows, in spite of their sensory onslaught, because of their clearly defined rules and structure. I knew there was a chance I might one day come to enjoy nights out on the town, but I would need to find the kind of spaces that worked for me.

Turns out, the slightly more hippy or theatrical areas of the rave scene in London hit that spot well for me, particularly as validating spaces to feel free and accepted as a trans woman.

Maybe it was in part the setting: venues with a lot more soft seating areas and colourful, welcoming decor. Maybe it was the wider range of ages and fashion sensibilities present that made the spaces feel more safe for self-expression. Maybe it was the fact you could see half the people in the room had eyes the size of dinner plates and were more than willing to make a new best friend for the night. But there was something about the hippy nightlife scene that instantly drew me in and made me feel at home.

Back when I first started going out raving in my mid-twenties, I did so a little cautiously. I would wear bright and colourful outfits; I certainly wasn't dressing to be invisible, but it was my first time presenting as female at events where people were probably not going to be sober, and I had a lot of anxiety about using gendered bathrooms. I know I have every right to use the women's bathrooms as a woman, but I'd had issues in the past with people trying to make me feel unwelcome in gendered spaces, and I wasn't sure if I could personally handle the prospect of that situation arising with someone who was perhaps heavily drunk and unwilling to be reasoned with.

I built the issue up a lot in my head, and those first few trips out raving I actively avoided using the bathrooms as much as possible, just in case. However, I didn't need to worry. Quite the opposite – nightclub bathrooms have been one of the most affirming places I have ever experienced for helping me feel confident about my appearance and style. Why? Well, because of the gender-affirming phenomenon of drunk-compliment girls.

A bit of a trope in pop culture, I had always assumed prior to my transition that the idea of a woman at a nightclub who gets a bit drunk and just gets the urge to tell strangers how beautiful and perfect they are was played up or exaggerated. I'd grown up around men, who for the most part never really expressed their feelings, regardless of their level of sobriety. At the very least, I never expected those women to be such a common part of going out and enjoying nightlife.

My very first time out raving, in the early hours of the morning, while waiting in a lengthy queue for a bathroom cubicle, the woman behind me in line tapped my shoulder to get my attention, just to spend several minutes telling me how gorgeous my hair was, asking what dye I used, complimenting my outfit, complimenting my smile, and just talking at length about how great a night I appeared to be having. Her energy was infectious, it felt completely sincere, and before I knew it, my self-confidence for the night was through the roof. This complete stranger had, out of the blue, made me feel amazing, and it was clearly done with no ulterior motive. This wasn't an attempt to hit on me, or to make me feel obliged to have a longer conversation. She was just drunk and really wanted me to know that my blue wavy hair reminded her of a mermaid, and that I would look amazing in a tiara as queen of the mermaids. It was ridiculous, and incredibly affirming.

And you know what? In the years since, this has become such a common experience on nights out, and it has had such an infectious impact on how I feel when going out that I've on occasion become that drunk-compliment girl myself. Sometimes I'll just hit that right kind of energy and feel the need to tell people at random how beautiful their outfit tonight is, or how lovely their hair looks. It's an oddly gendered experience, and one that has been a really big help in me having the confidence to wear adventurous outfits in places I know there will be people to see me.

Beyond getting drunk compliments on my hair from strangers in a club, venturing more confidently into late-night music events also led to another confidence-boosting and affirming experience: starting to get hit on by strangers, often straight men.

I've never really been attracted to men as much in practice as I am in theory. My sexuality is complicated to nail down; I'm mostly attracted to women, but there are occasional men who just tick all my boxes and blow me out of the strictly lesbian waters. Heavily femme-leaning pansexual might be the best term for me to use. I've been attracted to men in the past, I have dated men, but they're the exception rather than the rule.

Prior to my transition, and honestly during the first few years I was out, I never really felt very attractive. A lot of that was down to having issues with my body, and a lot of it was just a lack of confidence. I didn't get many compliments on my appearance, and online I actively faced waves of negativity any time I posted pictures of myself where I thought I looked cute. My experiences raving, and getting complimented on my appearance by the aforementioned drunk girls in the bathroom, were a big part of my growing self-assurance and, looking back, I think that increase in confidence got noticed.

When I finally started to get hit on during nights out it was often by the kind of straight men who do absolutely nothing for me, but honestly, that didn't even really matter that much. Everyone was respectful when I let them know I wasn't interested in them like that, but every time I got this really lovely hit of self-confidence which surged through me.

I know my sense of self-worth probably shouldn't be tied up in how other people view my appearance, but after years of being called an ugly old fat balding man on the internet by people who just don't like trans women existing, it was nice to know there were people who might spot me from across a room and decide they needed to come and introduce themselves to me. The fact they thought I was cute enough to single out was flattering in its own kind of way. Maybe it was the newness, or the novelty, but I came to feel a lot better about my appearance just as a result of a couple of strangers striking up conversations with cheesy, terrible pick-up lines.

It was nice to feel attractive at a time in my life where I was constantly being told I would never be as beautiful as a cis woman. I'm just thankful I was going on the kinds of nights out where I felt safe to turn people down without having to be too nervous.

Now, this story is all building up to probably the most body-confident night of my life, but a night that needs a little context to build up to.

One of the aspects of my body that I was most self-conscious about during my early transition was my breasts. They're a visibly obvious aspect of stereotypical gender presentation, and as someone who was desperate to be perceived as female by the world, a nice set of breasts seemed like a sure-fire way to get correctly gendered a good percentage of the time. I wanted breasts for myself and my own image of my body, but their impact on how other people would see me was a nice bonus I was excited about.

However, most trans women who start medical transition after a testosterone puberty end up with fairly small breasts. We naturally end up a couple of cup sizes below our family average, and most trans women will end up at most around an A- or B-cup bra size. I knew this in theory, I knew it in practice, but that still didn't prevent me feeling a bit disappointed with the first few years of my breast development.

From looking directly down, they looked really small. Granted, I've learned in the years since this is the worst angle for looking at your own breasts – they'll always look bad – but I was a bit insecure nonetheless. They were a bit of a sore spot in my self-image. I used to wear breast forms to pad out a bra and increase the perceived size of my chest, but those chicken-fillet bra inserts get hot and sweaty fast, and are a lot of hassle to wear. More than once I had one fall out while running for a bus, which is embarrassing as all hell.

So, back to my night of body positivity: I'd gone

out raving, and the event we were at just hit a very body-positive vibe. A lot of people were wearing little in the way of clothing, and everyone was being chill about it. Everyone was just on the vibe of 'bodies are awesome, let's show them off'.

At this point, my body positivity was probably at an all-time high. After months of nice drunken bathroom compliments and respectfully being hit on by strangers, I was in this room of people who didn't seem to care about everyone showing some skin, so I took the plunge. I took my top off and enjoyed a night of dancing, not worrying about the fact my breasts were fairly small.

The thing that most struck me as meaningful about that night was that at no point was I made to feel unsafe or unwelcome in gendered bathroom spaces. I wasn't any less a woman for my fairly small chest, and knowing that really helped me to dance off a lot of that baggage I had been carrying around for a while.

In the months and years that followed, I have become a lot more comfortable with my body, my small but still wonderful breasts included. I was never much one for nightlife, but the hippy rave scene ended up being a really big and important part of my journey to being able to see myself as beautiful just the way I already am.

The Radical Vulnerability of Trans Sex

Katherine Cross

A translatina writer, scholar and cat mom; she lives in Seattle with one of her partners

To feel safe in a lover's arms is to feel the touch of the Goddess – or God, if you're into that sort of thing. The desire for such safety is almost universal; for those who have no desire or need for lovers, other forms of companionship fulfil the need to be *known* yet safe all at once. What these experiences have in common is that they all embody a form of vulnerability. To reveal the entirety of one's self, or those parts that risk arousing shame and self-loathing, to another person is always a terrifying exercise – but the embrace of the revelation is the divine bit.

Like so much else in our irony-poisoned culture, that ancient insight has been memed. Writer Tim Kreider's *New York Times* essay on love culminated in a thesis that would go on to be widely quoted, both sincerely and in jest: 'If we want the rewards of being loved, we have to submit to the mortifying ordeal of being known.' There's something in the line's self-seriousness that seemed to beg for satire, like so much else in the *Times*'s culture pages. But such humour always hides the anxiety that earnestness threatens to reveal. Irony folds back on itself here: the joke is that we make jokes to *avoid* submitting to the mortifying ordeal of being known.

For trans people, to be vulnerable with someone invariably entails being out, to at least some degree. And there are few places one can be more mortifyingly out than in a lover's arms.

Talking about sex and sexuality as a trans woman remains impossibly fraught at times. Transmisogyny regards us as too masculine when it's convenient, and too feminine when it's not; thus a topless trans woman may be arrested for the 'indecency' of baring her breasts in public and then thrown in a men's jail for the alleged crime, while shirtless cis men may walk around freely. We are often bound by this double helix of contradictions in *consensual* sexual situations as well. For a trans woman to express pleasure in her own body, to have fetishes, is to be seen as either ill (what sane person would take pleasure in being a woman/trans?) or as a man (because only men get horny).

In a manoeuvre that should shock no one, male scholars tried to pathologise self-love among women – trans women specifically. Men like sexologist Ray Blanchard and psychologist J. Michael Bailey promoted the theory of 'autogynephilia' – literally 'love of oneself as a woman'. The argument was that transgender women

– especially those of us who were bisexual, lesbian, or otherwise not straight in our orientation – were actually extreme fetishists who transitioned because we got off on the very idea of being women. As biologist Julia Serano put it in a recent journal article:

> Autogynephilia ... not only invalidates trans women's gender identities (by misrepresenting them as 'men' who suffer from psychopathologies), but because it sexualises them – it reduces trans women to their presumed sexual behaviours and motivations, to the exclusion of other characteristics.[*]

Of course, femme people of all genders – whether cis or trans – can feel aroused by the sight of themselves. 'Feeling sexy' isn't exactly an esoteric experience, but for transgender women and many AMAB non-binary people it is sometimes apprehended as a pathological one. A mortifying ordeal indeed.

The theory of autogynephilia is easily disproved through recourse to sexological literature (or, in a rare experience for men of Blanchard's ilk, listening to a woman). Desire exists on a spectrum, weaving in and out of our genders and sexualities. It is laughable, at any rate,

---

[*]   Serano, Julia. 'Autogynephilia: A scientific review, feminist analysis, and alternative "embodiment fantasies" model'. *The Sociological Review*, 2020, 68(4), 763–78, available at journals.sagepub.com/doi/abs/10.1177/0038026120934690?journalCode=sora

to suggest that trans women would go through the trouble and risk of transition just to experience a little extra sexual pleasure.

But that doesn't mean we can't be turned on by ourselves, our bodies – and this is where one unlaces herself from the corset of respectability politics.

The classical narrative of trans existence, necessitated by decades of social and medical conservatism, demands that we be 'normal' in every way but for being 'born in the wrong body'. 'We're just like you' are words never addressed to queer people, Black and brown people, the poor, sex workers, or others. We are asked not to identify with the 'whores and the freaks', much less to want to *be* them. But I did not transition to be the model of demure femininity, ever available to men's whims; I transitioned to be myself. And, far from not playing a role in that self, sexuality was a huge part of it.

Most of us trans folk, regardless of our gender, have that awkward childhood experience – which stretches agonisingly into one's teens – where we are unsure whether we want to sleep with someone or *be* them. Most of my crushes, whether in school or on TV, were girls/women that, I realised with hindsight, I wanted to *be*. Some of this is the result of sexual sublimation. Being forced to be a boy means that sexual attraction is one of the only 'safe' (i.e. socially acceptable) ways to admire or express approval of a woman. But there was also an element of wanting to be a strong, commanding woman in all areas of my life. I wanted to be *Star Trek*'s Captain Janeway at school, at work *and* in the bedroom. I also learned that my body could be sexy in the way I aspired to, without having to hate myself in order to get there.

I learned all of this in the most *and* least unlikely place: *World of Warcraft*.

It's easy to mock erotic role-playing (ERP) in *World of Warcraft*, and it'd be richly deserved. Mine was no exception. Prose more purple than a rope bruise, scenarios so absurd they make the 'plumber coming over to lay some pipe' seem literary, and some kinks that are worth shaming at least a little (using Night Elf ears as dildos, for instance). But I don't judge, in truth. Everyone who's mocked the little town of Goldshire, a major ERP hub in *WoW*'s Elwynn Forest, has fucked there at least once – or thought about it in those dull hours between raids.

Yet the ERP was also eloquent in that way that only the drunk and unchained can be. The lawlessness was generative.

As players, we dragged each other into the dark corners of those dungeons and explored our digital bodies. Thus it was here along the unique, winding road of my life, I was introduced to futanari.

Futanari, Japanese for '[to be of] two kinds', is a term that was often used to describe 'androgyny', trans women's bodies, or to describe specific types of intersex people's bodies. The term was later appropriated by anime and hentai fans to describe trans women with penises. Similarly, in online gaming it was often employed as a slightly gentrified way of saying that one's female character happened to have a bit extra downstairs. When I ERPed with those people, letting my priestess get down on her knees to worship an altogether different goddess, I worked through feelings of disgust and shame.

It was a lovely coincidence that one of my more constant companions was themselves experimenting with that digital embodiment as a way of embracing their transmasculine identity. We were flaming trash barges passing in the night.

Eventually I moved from having my characters simply fellating 'futas' to becoming one myself, fucking my way to self-acceptance.

WoW's lore is quite malleable, you see: a world tree with limitless branches. It's a rubbish tree, strictly speaking, but a tree nonetheless. It admits so very many additions and reinterpretations that it seems tailor-made for fan culture and fanfic. Blizzard, the game's developer, made it abundantly clear that their lore is disposable. If Lord of the Rings' lore is written in stone, then WoW's is a collection of damp sandcastles in the shape of timeshares. It changes constantly to suit unfathomable whims – and if it's being taken that unseriously by Blizzard, who's to say a Druid can't fashion a dick for herself out of vines summoned from the Emerald Dream, or that a Paladin or Priest can't summon a 'shaft of Light' that is – innocently, of course – used to help infertile couples conceive? Suddenly my characters' genitals were as variable as their class spec. Before long, I was making my transmasc friend's character go down on *mine*, a stately Druidess who knew how to work leather.

Dear reader, it was such beautiful, beautiful garbage.

What I was left with, at any rate, was a towering sense of womanhood with a polyvocal body. Somewhere along the way, I came to accept that women's bodies were not what I had been told. The fantasy alchemised into an understanding of reality – *WoW* was where I met other trans women who opened my eyes to the possibility, however faint, that I too might transition – and I found myself alt-tabbing out of the game to visit tsroadmap.com (remember that site?) late at night. The link was helpfully supplied by the Night Elf warrior who put a collar on my priestess.

Before long, being a woman with a penis didn't seem like a contradiction. It felt plausible, normal *and* desirable. In *World of Warcraft* my simulated vulnerability quickly turned into the real thing; having a healthy sex life, however virtual, was the start of something more.

Through it all I felt positively roguish; I was hiding something from all these people, surely. What I didn't realise was how much I was revealing, how much of me was steadily becoming *known* night after night. To them, and to myself.

'Feeling like a woman' is shorthand for deeper mysteries that dwell far beyond the gender binary. It means keeping dysphoria at bay, it means not being seen as a man, and perhaps knottiest of all, it means feeling most like yourself. The latter is the tricky bit: it transcends the issue of dysphoria, for one thing. Averting dysphoria is merely a *precondition* for feeling like myself. The baseline. To feel like myself means for there to be some concordance between my self-image and what I am embodying in any given moment. That's where gender euphoria truly lies, and why it is not merely the opposite of *dys*phoria.

Through role-playing I developed some sense of the kind of person I wanted to become: a smart, strong-willed, witty woman. My different characters allowed me to explore different parts of myself: the overly optimistic side that struggles against naivete, the world-weary and experienced side of myself that teaches others, the wise-cracking side of me that uses humour as a defence mechanism. Each also opened the door, however slightly, to a new understanding of my sexual self. Obviously, I didn't transition to live out some fetish, but sexuality provided a safe space for regarding transition as even being *possible*. It also allowed me to slice through those mummifying layers of shame about my body, my desires, and the simple fact that I would have to transition.

With the erosion of shame also came the discovery that I was really into BDSM, but the experience of kink in an online erotic role-playing context is dramatically different from the physical reality of it. To do it well, one has to be vulnerable.

You have to learn to laugh during sex, first and foremost; this is something most popular media portrayals of sex do little to prepare you for.

You learn, the hard way, that however real a piece of media may feel, it exists in its own dream logic that bears only a passing resemblance to the embodied experience of what it portrays; much as Salvador Dalí's iconic melted pocket watch evokes but is decidedly *not* the real thing. That was what another much-memed piece of art was trying to teach us: René Magritte's *The Treachery of Images* wasn't just being wanky with its '*Ceci n'est pas une pipe*' caption. The portrayal isn't the thing it's portraying. The map is not the territory.

As I transitioned, the territory of my body was one that stubbornly refused to conform to the maps that existed, even the ones I'd hastily sketched on my ERP nights. Embracing that chaos, the joy of getting lost in myself with another became an unexpectedly fun part of the journey.

In her excellent *A Field Guide to Getting Lost*, historian Rebecca Solnit reminds us that the word 'lost' comes from Old Norse's *los*, the disbanding of an army. 'This origin,' she writes, 'suggests soldiers falling out of formation to go home, a truce with the wide world. I worry now that many people never disband their armies, never go beyond what they know.'

In the years since I transitioned, the times when I disbanded my armies were the most truly rewarding. And that disbanding came to be the only way I would know happiness in the arms of a lover, to truly know that safety through vulnerability.

A bookish trans writer who I scurried home with at 1 a.m., nuzzling each other as we waited for the 1 train at 96th Street, encouraging me to pull her hair when we crammed into her tiny bedroom; my current live-in partner teaching me what 'points of attachment' were as she lit candles to set the mood; another current partner guiding my girldick into her as we made a palace out of a San Francisco hotel that had seen better days. I could rhapsodise about each memory with the same prose that attended my ERP reflections, but the truth is that what made those moments beautiful was learning to laugh at each other.

When my girldick slipped *out* of my partner it was occasion for shared snickers rather than shame. When my lengthy tresses got in my mouth due to one head-bowed position or other, we'd sigh and joke about 'long-hair problems'. This is where sexuality merges with the comic that jokes the truest measure of love is asking your partner to see if you have butt warts. I could role-play being a sexy dominatrix who was always in control, a furious battle-mistress whose partners came in time to the lashings she gave, but the goofier reality was more fun, more authentic and, dare one say, more euphoric.

With my cis partners, meanwhile, the laughter was always mutual, joyous, a shared recognition of the absurdity that attended the practice of naked bodies grinding against one another; that truth, oft acknowledged, that sex is *hilarious*. The laughter was never at my expense; never once did I look in their eyes and see anything less than acceptance.

The sexual pleasure was, of course, delightful. But the vulnerability was the truly intoxicating thing. It was being known, yes, but well *past* the feeling of mortification. It was biblical knowledge. But the not-so-dirty secret is that that knowledge entails much that is neither sexual nor fetishised. Real BDSM entails office clips being used to hold a fraying pair of handcuffs together, awkward training from a random passer-by in a dungeon, careful conversations about boundaries interspersed with nerdy jokes, finding ways to turn a stuck zipper into a sexy dance then laughing together at the inevitable failure, and, finally, trusting that you're still going to have a good time anyway.

Those aren't the only moments when I feel most myself, of course, but we should reclaim sexuality as a site of power for ourselves, not only in all its luridness but also, perhaps especially, in its ridiculousness. I spent half a lifetime fearing laughter in such situations, only to realise it could be the surest sign of safety. If indeed safety in a lover's arms is the Goddess's touch, a lover's laughter is Her voice.

All of that can only be experienced when those armies are disbanded, when I can be lost and reveal myself as I truly am: not just trans, but an inveterate dork.

Being Daddy: Sex, Gender, Kink and Everything In Between

Mxtress Luna

Twenty-six, agender writer and sex worker
living in Aberystwyth, Wales

It's hard to be trans in the sex industry. It's especially hard to be pre-medical transition in the sex industry. It's even harder to be both those things and fat in the sex industry. I seem to have a huge number of labels that marginalise me. I'm a queer bisexual agender non-binary person who is disabled, schizophrenic, fat, poor and a full-service sex worker. I could also fit under the wider 'mentally ill' or 'transmasculine' labels. It sounds ridiculous even to me and I'm not sure how I ended up having to cope with so many things stacked against me. I have some big privileges too, though – I'm white, living in the UK, I have a master's degree and a home I can just about afford, as well as a job and a business to keep me busy. I enjoy my life. I'm blessed to be able to operate independently and I'm blessed to enjoy my jobs immensely. I work part time at a UK sex-worker charity while also running my own sex-work business. A lot of my life is taken up being immersed in one aspect or other of the sex industry.

So I have some oppression I can't help and I have some that I chose. I knew the stigma when I started sex work and I still made the happy decision to start. I was between the third year of my BA and the first year of my MA and I had a job in a shop that didn't pay enough for me to move house, which I had to do because the landlord said so. I needed £1,200 for a deposit, and first month's rent up front, and I was earning £150 per week. I had no time to save up, and ended up couch-surfing for six months before I found a room online I could have for £375 per month. The best part – the current tenant had already paid three months' rent in advance and they had to leave so urgently they didn't care if they never saw that money again. They were also happy to let me inherit the deposit they'd put down when they moved in. So no deposit required. Free rent for three months. Fuck, yes.

I started sex work online, but soon decided to start escorting instead. I didn't suit the webcam format, and figured I could make much more as a bona fide whore. Strangely, though, I never came out as transgender at my new job. I started under the name 'Luna' – a name that blends my hippy philosophy and classic sex-worker aesthetics perfectly. A name that's unmistakably feminine. I was partly under the impression that no transmasculine people did sex work (blatantly wrong) and partly trying to minimise the amount of work I had to put in to create my stage persona. I needed money; I needed to be popular; I sacrificed my transness for those causes.

It didn't work, though.

There's a certain amount of sex work that is just essentially lying. Whether it's inflating your earnings to show off, reducing your age, or telling a client who's paid for small-penis humiliation that his eight-inch schlong is a pathetic tiny worm. They're necessary lies that everyone tells. Clients expect it of us. It helps us maintain a bit of a difference between real life and work, because obviously we'd never bother telling these lies in real life. But at work we are our own product and we have to market ourselves – that means being the age clients want you to be. That means providing the paid-for service with a smile. That means presenting yourself as the best by any means necessary. All the other workers know what you're doing, and they do it too sometimes. I don't remember being told these rules, but it just became obvious after a while that that's how it works.

So I'm not sure why I couldn't continue lying about my gender.

I could have continued presenting as a cis woman at work, and probably had a much easier time of it, but I came out as non-binary after about six months. I changed my stage name to Mxtress Luna, and revelled in my new identity as a genderqueer kinkster who specialises in gender play. It seemed that my BDSM side worked perfectly with my regular identity, and I couldn't keep pretending to be cis while dressing men up in frilly knickers and stockings.

I was trans and therefore I was interested in gender play – not the other way round. I knew my clients usually felt a certain amount of shame about their proclivities, and I couldn't abide by that. I needed to reassure them there was nothing shameful or wrong about this, even if I acted like there was during the session. I decided I wanted to be a dominant for trans and gender-nonconforming people. I knew this would limit my capacity for mainstream success. I did it anyway. I wanted to do my part and be able to guide people through these feelings of shame and embarrassment and help them reach a truce with their gender identity. I couldn't see how a cis provider could do what I do without the first-hand experience of gender dysphoria or gender euphoria. I felt like these clients were part of my community and I wanted to care for them if they'd let me.

I came out as transgender when I was sixteen, but I'd known I was transgender for a long time before that. I'd been 'feeling' trans long before I knew there was a word for it, though. I was privileged to be accepted by everyone who mattered – my mum, dad, sister and close friends were all on my side, even if they didn't quite understand what that meant at the time. I was lucky to have so many good people around me, and I understood the value of community. I thought, *If nothing else, I can provide my clients with solidarity and a safe place to explore their feelings.*

When I met her, Princess was a guy interested in cross-dressing as a fetish. We had a few sessions where I'd describe turning him into a beautiful femme fuckdoll. It was my job to paint a picture of him as a hypersexualised Barbie, ready to be fucked and fulfil her duty at a moment's notice. We spoke regularly, though, not just about sex. We got along well, I was introduced to her cat (a beautiful black long-haired void baby), and we eventually got to negotiating a long-term relationship. I would receive regular 'tributes' (money) from her and we would talk almost daily, even if we were just checking in on one another. We have a genuine connection, and we promised to be the best versions of ourselves possible for each other. The only difference is we started this relationship in a transactional space, and I continue to take money from Princess whenever I want it. All I have to do is ask her. Sometimes she sends cash to surprise me and cheer me up.

So Princess ended up being a large part of my life from very early on in my sex-work career. I still am unsure whether it was wise for me to open up to her as much as I did, and I dread to think what could have happened if Princess had been someone more malicious. But she has always been honest and open with me, and I have always returned the favour. I've never had a more harmonious relationship, even before I started sex work. However, at work I am unabashed about setting clear boundaries and using straightforward language to express what I want or need. I have to do it because my safety depends on it. Before I started sex work, I wouldn't dream of using 'no' as a full, complete sentence.

I am a thousand times more confident denying, giving and withdrawing consent now than I was before I started sex work. As a teenager, I was sexually assaulted multiple times and could never muster the courage to say *anything*, let alone 'no'. I had boundaries pushed on a regular basis on everything from 'don't touch my hair' to 'get out of my bed'. I just didn't know how to communicate my discomfort, so I'd go along with it. I'd never say no to anyone about anything; I was a complete pushover in all aspects of my life. I was always lending money and giving out cigarettes, never asking for anything in return. I thought if I could be a low-maintenance friend I'd be more likely to be tolerated. They were never going to really like me, but at least they wouldn't dislike me.

Princess was my trial run of being 'demanding'. I don't think she knows it, but she allowed me to test drive my new, boundaried existence. I would practise asking for what I wanted on her, and she always gave me exactly what I wanted. I had lived so far with a mild sadistic streak and I knew, as far as BDSM was concerned, that I was a switch (that's someone who can be either submissive or dominant, and can switch between the two). All I needed was a space in which I was encouraged to be one. It changed my life and allowed me to let go of a lot of my past mistakes, which I made when I just wasn't capable of expressing my wants and needs. I forgave myself for allowing myself to be treated like a doormat. My Princess made that happen, and I'm not sure if she even knows what she did.

When Princess came out to me as transgender, I was so pleased for her. We'd spoken a lot about gender roles and expectations, and the ways we did and did not fit into the norm there. She knew I was trans and she knew the scenes I planned would be informed by that and designed to help her examine these parts of herself. I had a feeling she just needed that little nudge to understand who she was, and I was pleased it had worked and she had that certainty about herself now. Realising you're transgender is equal parts thrilling and terrifying. On the one hand, you finally have the vocabulary to describe yourself. You have absolute proof that you are not the only one who feels the way you've been feeling for God knows how long. You learn that the things you've idly dreamed about actually exist in real life if you know where to look. You learn that you can change how you look. It's a flood of relief and a sense of belonging that changes your entire world view. On the other hand, there's no way you don't know what they do to people like us. You've got a new shiny target painted on your back and the only way to get rid of it is to lie and hide who you are indefinitely. Even then it might not work. Is it worth the stigma and violence you expose yourself to? We both decided yes, it is.

When I first came out as trans, I identified myself as a trans man, FtM, dude boy manly man. I think just learning that there was an option to be another gender made my pendulum swing as far away from feminine as it could, as a knee-jerk reaction. I cut all my hair off, bought a binder and wore it constantly – I'd even sleep in it. I also embarked on a mission to own every single plaid shirt the world ever made, sometimes with a waistcoat too. I enjoyed being unusual; I enjoyed the confrontations with bigots. I was a man and that meant I was allowed to take up space and be loud and vulgar and assertive. It was a little bit of a power trip, but ultimately it wasn't for me. I struggled to emulate the cis men around me because I wasn't sure they were worthy of being emulated. I gravitated towards kinder, softer-spoken men who have an unconcealed caring heart.

The long and short of it is that I looked at and studied and thought about gender and gender roles so much and for so long that they lost all meaning to me. In exactly the same way that if you say a word too many times in a row, it ceases sounding like a real word at all. It's called semantic satiation and it ruined my perception of gender for ever. I've examined every piece from tone of voice to gait to language patterns and I can't work out how to reconfigure the elements into 'male' and 'female' any more. They all fit in to every box, and I get genuinely confused when a cis person tries to assume I know how they think gender works, because it just no longer makes sense to me. I blew my gender fuse.

But one day I learned to grasp one of those elements and hold on tight to it. The day Princess called me Daddy. It's a cliché that sex workers (especially kinky ones) have daddy issues – and also, mostly, just untrue. However, as a dominant, I realised my style was masculine yet loving. I was a protector and a guide to my Princess and loved her the way you love family. I had taken on some of the role of Daddy, and for the first time a gendered perception stayed firm in my mind.

I know some of those unable to disconnect BDSM from sex are sucking their teeth, imagining some hard-core incest fantasy scene between a father and daughter, but that's not the meaning of being Daddy to me. I'm Daddy outside of the bedroom mostly in totally non-sexual ways. I commiserate and congratulate, I help plan grand plans and then help execute them. I do all the things a father does, while simultaneously loving and accepting Princess for the trans person she is. That makes me warm and fuzzy. That, as a gender role? That fits me like a warm knitted jumper passed down through the family.

Being Daddy to me means being loving, nurturing and soft. It means being a hard ass when someone's being an idiot, and talking someone round from a dumb decision. It means protecting and caring for your family. It means doing some of the crappy chores no one else wants to do. It means lending a hand and a listening ear. It means getting to be the living continuation of my dear, departed father. It means continuing his legacy and taking in waifs and strays and helping out where I can.

My gender euphoria is a birth rite.

Acknowledgements

Thank you to my partners, Jane and Pheonix, for putting up with me vanishing for long periods of time to work on this book, and for their love and support during the writing process.

Thank you to all of this book's contributors, who shared their stories and made this book what it is today.

Thank you to everyone who shared this book when we first announced it, and who supported our crowdfunding campaign. Your support allowed this project to get off the ground.

And thank you to everyone who has taken the time to read this book. I hope that you feel as much joy reading it as I did working on its creation.

Unbound is the world's first crowdfunding publisher, established in 2011.

We believe that wonderful things can happen when you clear a path for people who share a passion. That's why we've built a platform that brings together readers and authors to crowdfund books they believe in – and give fresh ideas that don't fit the traditional mould the chance they deserve.

This book is in your hands because readers made it possible. Everyone who pledged their support is listed below. Join them by visiting unbound.com and supporting a book today.

Cameron Ax
James Aylett
Magdalena Azmitia
Tiffany B R
Karo B.
Quinta B.
Lucy Bailey
Manon Bailly
Sian Bain
Josephine Baird
Em Baker
Ethan Baker
Gemma Baker
Katelin Baker
Mathias Baker
Michael Baker
Tony Baker
Rachel Barber
Quinn Barbuta
Nichole Barger
Austin Barnes
Michelle Barnett
Janine Barnett-Phillips
Henry James Barnosky
Christopher Barrett
Jacob Bartynski
Gage Batchelder
Ezra Batt
Ada Bean
Riley Bean
Jake Beardsley
Rebecca Beardsley
bears
Lucy/Lee Beaumont
Laura Beaupain
Emily Bell
George Bell
Jessica Bellon
Winter Belmont
Deem Belozerco
Joseph Benner
Louis Benzing
Richard Berd
Christopher Berg
Biadora
Mads Birch
Brent Black
Sam Blanchard
Jack Blanke
Roisin Blanks
Astra Bloom

Jo Bloom
Steff Böckenholt
Rachel Boddice
Becky Bolton
Roslyn Bolton
Dorothy Bonita
Enfys Book
Willow Bostock
Inari Bourguenolle
Zoë Bourque
Sara Bovi
Tom Bowers
Ed Bracey
Becca Bradford
David J Bradley
Kate Bradley
Alex Brailsford
Holly Branch
Jaime Breeden
Kiera Brennan
David Breutzmann
Kirsten Breve
Mark Bridge
Adrian Briggs
Ben Briggs
Kelly Bright
Zachary Brill
Gaz Brocklebank
Jan Broekhuizen
Emma Brookes
Mark Brown
Morgan Brown
Sam Brown
Sarah Brown
Bobby Bruce
Kat Brunette
Piia Brusi
Kay Buchanan
Yvonne Budden
Erika Bui
Annen Buranen
Lucy Burba
Taylor Burch
Patrick Burden
Erwin Burema
Emily Burgardt
Violet Elizabeth Burgert
Cassandra Burn
Mikhael Johannes Burnard
Andrew Burns
Josh Butler

Kai Butler
Naomi Byrne
Pia C
Andrea Cabral
Gabriel Cabrera Flores
Asteria Caesar
Nikola Calik
Liam Callaghan
Simon Callan
Jessica Camgros
Andrew Campbell
Jake & Charlie Campbell
Michael Campbell
Nora Canby
Ryan Cannon
Fox Caporgno
Grace Carman
Tegan Carney
Tobias Carroll
Alex Carter
Dare Cascado
Kate Cassidy
Ryan Castellucci
Alison Castle
Ollie Chamberlain
Alex Chan
Marceline Chapman
Finlay Charlton
Zoe Chatfield
CheshireBeast
Jean Chickenby
Abbey Childs
Chip
Raymond Chira
Alex Choudhary
Chris Christie
Amira Chuka
Alexander Clark
Colin Clark
Danielle Clark
Jeff Clark
Madeline Clark
Morgan Clark
Ryan Clark
Charli Clement
Lauren Clinnick
Lindsey Cobb
Thea Cochrane
Alec Cohen
Maple Colburn
Tabitha Cole

Theo Colley
Anastasia Colman
Frederik Colpman
Amy Conkerton-Darby
Sean Conklin
Brooke Connell
Hari Conner
Frankie Conyers
Parley Cook
Jessica Cooper-Smith
Noah Cooperider
Trevor Coote
Joseph Cordery
Lauren Corsaut
August Cotter
Kristofer Couch
Will Cowley
E Cox
Joanne Cox
Ashlee Craft
Nathaniel Crain
Kayleigh Crawford
Sal Creber
Crime Bird
Matthew Crockett
Kira Cross
Peter Crouch
Kendra Crow
Lucie Crowe
Mary R. Crumpton
Eri Cruz
Brandon Cruzen
Charlie Cullen
Jennifer-Lee Cullen
Max Cummings
Amanda D'Andrea
Renee D'Netto
Damien Da Silva
Michaela Dalbert
Jenny Dale
Chance Dan
Maya Dancey
Sammuel Dandrea
A Daniels
Kayla Daspit
Lia Davey
Beth Davidson
Charlotte Davies
Mattie Davies
Rose Davies
Deanna Davis

Ivy Davis
Mindy Davis
Theresa Davis
Christopher Dawson
Seph De Busser
Sanaya Deas
Parker Armando Deckard
Christian DeCoster
Jason DeFontes
Mia del Barrio
Ash Demetriou
Niamh Dempsey
DenDen / Zoë
Joe Denison
Andrey Denisov
Steph Sabriel Sarah
    Denney
David Devlin
Rachael Dewhurst
Michael Dickson
Samuel Dixon
Magda Dlugaj
Matthew Dobler
Josephine Doe
Eloise Doehren-Tierney
Rain Doggerel
Sara Domanski
Kassandra Dominguez
Joanna Douglas
Alice Dowhyj
George Downward
Ginger Drage
April Drees
Ezilia Dring
Bruce Driver
Josiah Drosendahl
Jackie Dubil
Liana Duffy
Hannah Duncan
Taylor Duncan
Amy Dunham
Robert Dunphy
Monika Durbin
Rob Durbin
Charlie Dutton-Sedman
Andrea Dworkowski
Asia Dyer
A E
Emily Eadie
Rob Eagle
Sarah Eales

Nicholas Eames
Jamie East
Celyn Ebenezer
Seth Echelbarger
Avery Edge
Emma Edwards
Hannah Ege
Sam Ehret
Sam Einhorn
Ami & Kurt Eitzen
Erin Ekins
Jacob Ela
Kevan Elkins
Autumn Ellington-Lewis
Julia Elliot
Syd Elmose
Imogen Ely
Jamie Emmott
Mary Ennis
Caeth Eri
Rozaline Ellie Escobedo
Espiox
Ilana Estreich
Finn Evans
Zack Evans
Melissa Eveleigh
Brendon Everett
F
Amy Farish
Kit Farmer
Lexi Farmer
Carwyn Farnham
Leo Farrell
Jade Farris
Zakia Fawcett
Keru Faye
Abi Fellows
Aiden Feltkamp
Christina Ferguson
Sirka Ferrin
Natalie Fiertz
Nico Figueroa
Adrianne Filart
Rebecca Finndell
Elizabeth Nia Finnegan
Seth Finnegan
Carmen Finnigan
Fiona
A Firth
Artie Firth
Madison Fisher

AJ Fitzwater
Sorella Fleer
Jeri Flowers
Ana Fluegel
Eimear Flynn
Julius Foitzik
Lee Foland
Libby-Mae Ford
Helen Forrest
Val Fortin
Amber Fox
Chris Fox
Eriol Fox
Jimmy Francis
Susan Francis
D Franklin
Pia Frankton
Vincent Freeland
Katie Freeman
Julia Freewoman
Ina Fried
Dawson Friesen
Bridget Frost
Robin Fry
Brandon Gagne
Jade Gaillard
Mar Galizio
Tino Galizio
D M Gallagher
Megan Gallagher
Mitchell Gallagher
Nick Gallego
Isabelle Gambardella
Alexis Garcia
Sarah Garcia
Kassandra Gardner
Frazer Gault
Stéphanie Gauvin
Denise Gawron
Claire Genevieve
T George
Johan Georgsson
Xenia Gilbert
Max Gilreath
Charlotte Gislam
Kel Gitter
Jennifer Glassmire-Policari
Amanda Glasspoole
Ylva Gløersen
Ryan Glover
Theo Glover

Marian Go
Volker Göbbels
Amanda Goertzen
Marco Gohl
Dave Gold
Brian Gomoll
Zachary Good
Keladry Goodell
Evelyn Goodman
Eva Goodrich
Madeline Goodwin
Rebecca Gorman
Elyas Gorogo-Baker
Julie Gough
Hannah Rose Govan
Daniella Graham Stollery
Terence Grainger
Jacob Grando
Idun Granrå
Signe Rhea Grau
　Kristensen
Ally Gray
Gray
Richard Graylin
Grayson
Thomas Grebenchick
DK Green
Rachel Green
Rebecca Green
Aaron Greenberg
Kaoru Greendrake
Faye Greenslade
Alt Greenwood
James Gregory-Monk
Rhys Grey
Victoria Grieve
Em Griffith
Baptiste Grob
Hattie Grünewald
Jennifer Gubernath
Katy Guest
Duke Guijt
Gregory Gustavsen
LP Guterman
Harriet H
Lena Hackworth
Jayce Ham
Henrik Viking Hansen
Nick Hansen
Lisa Harald
Emma Harcourt

Ell Harman
Dani Harmon
Jasmin Harper
Becca Harper-Day
Robynn Harris
Ema Harrison
Toni Harrison
Laurie Hartley
Mari Hartman
Jeremy Harvey
Sarah Hasselman
Hastie
Chloe Hawes
Harrison Healey
Jason Healy
Keir Healy
Tierra Healy
Benjamin Heap-Webster
Benjamin Heath
Brooke Heathcock
Jennifer Jane Heaton
Samuel Hedley
Liana Hedlund-Drumm
Erwin Heemsbergen
Michael Heffernan
Margaret Grace Heidel
Joshua Heming
Forrest Henry
Karen Henson
Anna Hepworth
Rox Herrington
Liam Heß
Angelina Hewitt
River Hibbs
Jen Hickman
Sean Hickman
Amy Hicks
Nic Higginbotham
Kaitlin Hilinski
Lu Hilmoe
Alex Hilton
Serena Hiner
Sarah Hipple
Hips
Perry Hirst
Lucien Hoare
Ed Hoc
Charlotte Hockey
Hannah Hodge
Alex Hodgson
TJ Hoffer

Katherine Hogben
Selena Hogg
Tessa Holcomb
HL Holder-Brown
Mi L Holliday
Holly
Kaylin Holmes
Ruth Holt
Emmeline Holwell
Jinx-Jae Hood
Tegan Horan
Em Hornbeck
Patrick Hoskin
Craig Houston
Meredith Howard
Abigail Howe
Henry Howe
Lauri Howes
Mitch Hubner
Charlie Hudson
Layla Hudson
Chris Hulbert
Hedy Hume
Finn Humphris
Andrew Hunt
Katie Hunt
Peyton Hunter
Sparrow Hurd
Martin Hush
Lizzie Huxley-Jones
Max Iarocci
Felix Ihle
Martin Ireland
Irie
Isabelle
Maggie Jack
Debbie Jackson
Judith Jackson
Claire Jadis
Jordan James
Keld James
Jarnope
Matthew Jenkins
Sophie Jennings
Jo
Sugar Joe
Katrina Johns
Tessa Johns
Matthew Johnston
Anatole Jolly
Jon

Jayesephine Jones
Lila Jones
Margaret Jones
Mark Jones
Nicholas Jones
Reece Jones
David Jovanovic
Sarah Jurado
Leah Karge
Cat Karskens
Nick Katers
Rebecca Kath
Jared Kayle
Seán Kearney
Adam Kelley
E.J. Kelly
Alex Kemp
Nicholas Kenny
Susan Kersten
Keshi
Sam Kevern
Jordan Khan
Jared Kidd
Scout Kientop
Dan Kieran
Rachel Anne Kieran, PsyD
Mira Kim
AJ King
Daniel King
Rowan King
Stephen King
Kit Kinney
Sagan Kirk
Thomas Klein
Tom Knight
Sarah Knowles
Kellie Kohler
Kana Kong
Rebecca König
Bronia Korabinska
Miko Kotek
Emily Kotre
Mana Kouwenberg
Jade Kovac
Cj Kral
Aisha Krause
Ellena Krčmář
Maxine Krebs
Cassandra Kremel
Jóhann Kristófer
Vsevolod Kritskiy

Shaun Kronenfeld
Rose Kuehr-McLaren
August Kulas
Nicola Kumar
Christina Kutscher
Pyrrh L
Olivia L.
Edith Lagos
Faye Lai
Teemu Laitinen
KJ Lamb
Chloe Lampard
Sophie Lane
Lia Langman
Fred Langridge
Trucy Lanthier-Rogers
Chris Larmouth
Jack Latona
Fion J. Lau
Signe Laursen
Sarah Lausen
Clara Lauterwasser
Gregory Lauzon
Madelyn Lawrence
Jupiter Lawson
Sarah Leaman
Jay Lee
Liisbet Leemets
Emma Leishman
Skye Lemme
Fox Lemmon
Caelum Lenchner
Kayla Lent
CJ Levine
Kelly Levy
Beth Lewis
Jake Lewis
Kira Lewis
Yvonne Lewis
Dana Lexa
Caroline Licitra
Aroa Likona
Georgia Lillie
Chris Limb
Aster Lindberg
Linus Lindblad
Jocelyn Link
Jay Livingston
Jamie LocPort
Sarah Locus
Sarah Longshaw

Dan Looker
Fatima Lopez
Jessica Lopez
Martina López
Munin Lorekeeper
Monica Lorentz
Jasper Love
Princess Carla Love
John Lozo
Samuel Ludford
Lebannen Luitreath
Jose Miguel Vicente Luna
Polina M
Rory M
Natalie M.
Rowan MacBean
Margo MacDonald
Rebekah Machemer
Saga Mackenzie
Ellie Mackin Roberts
James Macleod + Charlie Wilson
Matthew Macomber
Jane Magnet
Adam Maidment
Catherine Makin
Marianthi Makra
Dan Malear
A B Mallory
Ryan Maloney
Q Rae Manning
A Mansion
Xian Mao
Moriarty Marchany
Lee Marie
Chris Marks
Madeleine Marrin
Jimmy Marsden
Cameron Marsh
Jamie Marshall
Alma Marstein
Joelle Martin
Lucy Martin
Nyani-Iisha Martin
Zoe Martin
Catherine Mason
Ryan Mason
Steve Mason
Deezy Matas
Katie Mather
Kit Matthews

Sophie Matthews
Rebecca Maughan
Indigo Maughn
Arthur Maurici
Michela May
Jameson Mayes
Fran Mazetto
Cathal Mc Ginley
Ethan McAlpin
Rita McAuliffe
Ashleigh Blair McConville
Ally McCrae
Anna McCue
Kellie McDonald
Laura McDonald
Abby McGrath
Kieran McGreen
Jennifer McInnes Winning
Kelly McKinley-Ford
Daniel Mclaughlan
Melanie McLean
Oisín McMahon
HD McMinn
Peter McMinn
Cian McNamara
Victoria McNamara
Evan McNiff
Chloe McParlin-Jones
Jon McPartland
Benny Mcsassy
Emilie McSwiggan
Elliot McVeigh
Ellen Mellor
Melme
Carl-Eric Menzel
Matthew Mesley
Neil Meyer
Jost Migenda
Ed Mikucki
Peter Miles
Emili Milinković-Stevenson
Codey Miller
Kayla Miller
Phillip Miller
Millie
Freya Milligan
Peter Mills
Torb Lunde Miranda
Nanashi Mitame
Bryan Mitchell
Celeste Mitchell

John Mitchinson
Kit Mitton
Kaajal Modi
Andrew Molloy
Zoey Monroe
Vincent Monster
Dee Montague
Heidi Moore
Jessica Moore
JL Moore
Jocelyn Moore
Mirco Moretti
Morgan & Roland
Justin Morgon
Grace Morley
Harley Marie Morrigan
Fionnuala Morris
Izzy Morris
Maxine Morris
Daniel Morrison
Elaine Morrison
Laura Morrison
Niamh Morrison
Tara Morse
Alia Mortada
Bobby Moss
Josh Mosteit
Chase Moudry
Sara Moura
Cassandra Mouratidis
Guinnevere Moydan
Charlotte Moyes
Craig Moyle
Theodore Muenster
Kristen Muenz
Darragh Mulcahy
Sara Mulkerrin
Melanie Munguia
Kavish Munjal
Josh Munro
Amber Murdock
Shaun Murphy
David Murray
Katie Myers
myrialux
Kristen Naegle
Carlo Navato
Eliane Neilson
General Nekosho
Kallie Nelson
Anne Nerison

SUPPORTERS

Nerra
Riley Finn Ness
Luci Nevins
Briony Newbold
Rob Newstead
Josie Newton
Leighton Newton
D Ní Chúirc
Natalie Nichols
Aer Nicholson Clasby
Freya Nicolson
Lily Echo Niehaus
Kes Nielsen
Drew Niewoehner
Taylor Nixon
Angus Noble
Blake Noble
Delia Noble
Madeline Noble
Martyn Noble
Hope Noel
Daria Noemi
Sisu Nojonen
Sally Noonan
Johannes Nordqvist
Vid Norene
Paula Norris
Space Northpaw
Sami Novaster
Ian Nowell
Victoria Nunez
Sonja Nyvoll
Melody Nyx
Laura O'Brien
Ellissa O'Connell
Brodie O'Connor
Jack O'Connor
Rob O'Donoghue
Jenny O'Gorman
Steve O'Gorman
Caitlin O'Loughlin
Kate O'Rafferty
Carleigh Obrochcta
Charlie Ocean
Jude Offord
Amory Oliver
Jennifer Ollett
Bremen Ortega
Amber Osborn
Ares Osborn
Alice Oseman

Evelyn Osman
Juan Osorio
Ada Ostrokol
Cameron Ostroot
Charlotte Owen
Sydney Pacione
Camilla Marie Pallesen
Dan Palmer
Eli Palmer
Robert Palmer
Nicolas Palumbo
Sumeet Panchal
Alyssa Pappas
Izzie Paragas
Em Rose Parker
Nikita Parks
Carlin Parry
John Parry
Sarah Passingham
Evie Patmore
Emery Patterson
Morgan Paulett
Alyssa Paxton
Thomas Pedersen
Fran Penney
Lowenna Penny
Jack Perkins
Lucy Perreault
Emily Perry
Holly Petch
Sonder Peters
Maddie Peterson
Eleanor Peyreton
Lawrence Phillips
Ryan Phillips
Bran Phillips-Lewis
Olivia Phipps
phyphor
Jackie Physics
Dave Pickering
Sabrina Pickering
Henry Pierpoint
Storm Pilloff
Renate Plehwe
Shane Darice Plumer
Eden Plummer
Wojciech Podgórni
Justin Pollard
Dimi Pollock
Nathaira Polyanarchist
Erin Pomidor

Graves Ponce
Julia Poole
Kara Potts
Caroline Povolny
Beth Powell
Matthew Powell
Stacey Powell
Roz Powers
Amy Powis
Ravi Pradhan
Rhianna Pratchett
Kara Presbrey
Kylee Price
Marc Price
Tina Price-Johnson
Nick Psyhogios
Laura Pugh
Ana Purcaroiu
Quinn
Lily Raffaele
Martin Ramsay
Zoe Rand
Raptorbricks
rash
Inanna Ravenscroft
Patrick Reames
Nina Recchia
Rosalina Reda
El Redman
Maeve D. Reese
Lydian Reeves
Louise Reid
Natalie A Reisenleiter
Justin Renchen
Luke Retallic
Maya Reter
Andrea Reynolds
Matt Chai Reynolds
Rhys Reynolds
Heloise Rhodes
Omi Rhodes
Thomas Rhodes
Cade Richard
Amy Richards
Owen Rickard
Neal Rideout
Willa Riggins
Anna Riley
George W. Rimmer
Pamela Ritchie
Bridgette River

SUPPORTERS

Catherine Roberts
Ioan Roberts
Robin Roberts
Andrew Robinson
Daniel Robinson
Molly Robison
Ed Robson
Sophie Robson
Muhammad Iqbal
    Rochman
J Rodland
Z.L. Rosato
David Rose
Jade Elliot Rose
Darcy Ross
Laura Roth
Correl Roush
Eleanor Rueger
Tess Rugg
Faye Russell
Jonathan P. Russell
Terry P. Russell
Hannah Rutherford
Efea Rutlin
Forrest Ryan
Alex Ryder
Sophie S.
Jed Sabin
Saer
Alex Saladrigas
Grace Salay
Eric Sanchez
Felix Sanchez Klose
Lindsay Sánchez Navarro
Terriss Sandberg
Erin Sanders
Sara
Taylor Saranic
Rachel Sargent
Tom Sargent
Atticus Schaedel
Jenna Schaefer
Jude Schick
Sibel Schick
Jenn Schiffer
Annie Nate Schindler
Nathaniel Schmitt
Mark Schoon
Lucia Schulze
Aubrey Scott
Joseph Scourfield

Tara Searle
William Seelhoff-Ely
Hayden Seen
Ruby Sefen
Grayson Semmens
Emily Senft
Chloe Senoussi
Teslynn Set
Seth
Sam Sewell
M Shaffer
Lizzie Shane
Sam Shatz
Aria Shaw
Sophie Shay
Kai Sheehan
Isobel Sheene
Aprile Shen
Lou Sheridan
Audrey Shilts
John A L Short
Jennifer Shuman
Kassandra Siegel
Finn Siegmund
Elizabeth Siemer
silhouby
Eric Silva
Jules Silveira
Silvia
Ellie Simmons
Sadie Simmons
Bryn Sinclair
Chris Sinjakli
R H Sinkins
SJR
Charles Skeavington
Roxanne Skelly
Gedi Skog
Gabriela Skrzeczkowska
Jupiter Eden Skye
Jake Slater
Anja Smith
Ben Smith
Cam Smith
Dominic Smith
John Smith
Lee Smith
Yel Smith
Brody Ryan Snedden
Lilliana Snow
M Solé

Eamon Somers
Luna Sophia
May Sophia
Kyle Sorenson
Ash Sorrel Holland
Allie Sousa
Axel Sparrow
J Spence
Cassandra Spencer
Luke Spencer
Synneva Spittel
Sarah Spruce
Wendy Staden
Alex Staehler
Megan Stags
Sam Standen
Ashley Stapleton
Stargirl
Carter Starkey
Sean Steele
Aubyn Stewart
Em Stewart
Alexander Stimson
Meg Stivison
Jayne Stockton
Rachel Stockton
Susanne Stohr
Lois Stone
Amy Kara Stonehouse
Nick Streeter
Koda Strider
Amanda Strnad
Dan Stuart
Michael Sugerman
Aidan Summers
Aidan-Astrid Summers
Emma Sunshine
Zawadi Svela
May Swinton
Jada Sylvest
Roxy Sylvester
Sarah Symon
Samantha Syvret
Nulani t'Acraya
Eryck Tait
Tako, Enthusiast
Tallulahhh
Ana Tanevska
Ramona Tanner
A Tate
Emma Taylor

Margaret Tedford
Melle Teich
Will Templeton
Juliana Teoh
Jay Thatcher
theimpliedbear
Oracle Thessia
Shannon Thoman-Black
Professor Ben Thomas
Ariel Thompson
Shelley Thomson
Tabitha Tipper
Leslie Rose Titze
Jefferson Toal
Jalen Todd
Edwyn Tolmie
Lara Torison
Marion Tout
Isabelle Tranner
Heather Traver
Julian Trettenes
Sascha Tripp
Else-Marie Trønnes
Holly Daisy Túlipa Adeyna
    Pumpkin
Lilly Tupa
Adrasteia Turing
Abby Turner
Joe Turner
M Turner
Stevie Turner
Joe Tutterow
Tyler
Stefanie Ulrich
Valentyn
Lyall Valk
Lena van Hale
Samara Adora van
    Harmelen
Rachel Suzie Vancleave
Anna Vanhinsbergh
Kris VanHoutte
Mathilde Vantorre
Nick Vaudrain
Tori Vaz
Sami Veillard
T Venczel
Carla Maus Ventzke
Max Veryan
Zac Veryard
Marion Vestheim

Axelle Vidal
Kai Villa-Vercella
Gina Villano
Pascal Vine
Sharon Vinson
Lilith Vinter
Christine Violet
Alice Violett
Johannes Vitzthum
Freja Volfing Højager
Marth von Loeben
Daniel von Schilgen
Aura Lily Vulcano
Kara Waalkes
Millie Wadkin
Oda Wahlstrøm Tolsrød
Charlie Wain
Branwen Walker
Jamie Walker
Ryan Walker
Jonni Wallace
Nadia Wallace
Victoria Walsh
Rowan Walters-Brunt
Chris Warburton
Ali Ward
CJ Ward
Aurora Nicole Wargmo
Will Warhurst
Ludo Waters
Marie Watkins
Katie Watts
★Adam J Waugh★
Anna Weaver
Matthew Webb
Brian Webber
David Webster
John Wells
Erin Wenban
Wendy & Josie
Timothy
    "KingIsaacLinksr"
    Wetzel
Marin Whebby
Adi White
Jordan White
Richard Whittaker
Charlotte Whittam
Holly Whitter
Rebekah Wild
Haley Williams

Winowa Williams
Kieran Miles Williamson
Arcade Willis
Avery Willis
Jake Willis
Johanna Wilson
Andi Wingate
Parker Wingate
Sarah Winters
Kris Wise
Nastassja Wiseman
Gretchen Woelfle
Ian Wolf
Jes Wolfe
Rachel Wolfe
Thomas Wolfe
Zoë Wolfe
Abigail Wood
Alex Wood
Lara Woolford
Donna Worby
Alexandros Worgan
Zachary Worley
Violet Zoë Wren
Amanda Wright
Kale Wright
Liz Wright
MJ Wright
WX
Shane Yach
Lauren Ybarra
Jessica Yopp
Billy Young
Josie Young
Telyn Z.
Julie Zeraschi
Rayne Zukas
Άννα Τσαγγαδά